Donna Reed

Donna Reed

A Bio-Bibliography

Brenda Scott Royce

Bio-Bibliographies in the Performing Arts, Number 16
JAMES ROBERT PARISH, Series Adviser

GREENWOOD PRESS
New York • Westport, Connecticut • London

Library of Congress Cataloging-in-Publication Data

Royce, Brenda Scott.
  Donna Reed : a bio-bibliography / Brenda Scott Royce.
    p.   cm. — (Bio-bibliographies in the performing arts, ISSN
  0892-5550 ; no. 16)
    Includes bibliographical references and index.
    ISBN 0-313-26806-1 (alk. paper)
    1. Reed, Donna, 1921-1986.   2. Reed, Donna, 1921-1986—
  Bibliography.   3. Motion picture actors and actresses—United
  States—Biography.   I. Title.   II. Series.
  PN2287.R285R69   1990
  791.43'028'092—dc20
  [B]   90-44109

British Library Cataloguing in Publication Data is available.

Library of Congress Catalog Card Number: 90-44109
ISBN: 0-313-26806-1
ISSN: 0892-5550

First published in 1990

Greenwood Press, 88 Post Road West, Westport, CT 06881
An imprint of Greenwood Publishing Group, Inc.

Printed in the United States of America

The paper used in this book complies with the
Permanent Paper Standard issued by the National
Information Standards Organization (Z39.48-1984).

10 9 8 7 6 5 4 3 2 1

Copyright Acknowledgments

The author and publisher gratefully acknowledge permission to use the
following:

Excerpts from Mason Wiley and Damien Bona, *Inside Oscar: The
Unofficial History of the Academy Awards.* Courtesy of Ballantine Books, a
Division of Random House, Inc., copyright © 1986.

Excerpts from Jeanine Basinger, *The "It's a Wonderful Life" Book.*
Courtesy of Alfred A. Knopf, Inc., copyright © 1986.

Excerpts from Tom Seligson, "Everybody's Mom." Reprinted with permission from Parade, copyright © 1985.

This book is dedicated to my mother,
Phyllis Jane Royce,
an unconventional Donna Reed.

Contents

Preface

Rather than a full-scale biography, this book is intended as a comprehensive reference to Miss Reed's career for use by researchers as well as fans. A brief biography is followed by detailed examinations of her work in motion pictures, television and radio. Media reviews of her work are listed in these sections, following the particular film or appearance being reviewed. Following these career sections is a listing of awards and nominations given to Donna Reed, and a chronology of major events in her life. The annotated bibliography covers all articles and items other than reviews printed about Miss Reed in major magazines, fan magazines, books and newspapers.

The entries in each of these sections are labeled for ease in cross-referencing throughout the book. All entries in the Filmography, for example, begin with the letter "F," and are numbered consecutively in chronological order (F1 through F40). The notation "see F14" in another section of this book would prompt the reader to look up that particular film for more information. Similarly, television appearances are assigned reference numbers preceded by a "T," radio appearances "R," awards and nominations "A," and bibliographical references "B." A listing of the 274 episodes of "The Donna Reed Show" is incorporated into the Television Appearances section, labeled DR1 through DR274.

The subject index, which concludes this book, uses the above described reference numbers for its entries as well as page numbers for references in the biography or other sections which are not numbered. For example, an entry reading "Doe, John, 12, F10, R13" would direct the reader to page 12, to the tenth film in the Filmography and the 13th listing under Radio Appearances for more information on Mr. Doe.

Donna Reed has been called "America's Favorite Mother" and her recognition as such has stood the test of time. Even today, on a national peanut butter commercial, when a young mother discovers that the brand she gives her children is not the best, she sighs, "So I'm not Donna Reed." The name "Donna Reed" alone conjures up the image of perfection in the roles of wife and mother.

But before she became known as ultimate mother Donna Stone on "The Donna Reed Show," Donna Reed was a veteran film actress with nearly forty films to her credit. Most prominent among these are It's a Wonderful Life and From Here to Eternity. Cast against type in the latter, she played the prostitute Alma, and her exceptional performance won her an Academy Award.

The high points of Donna Reed's career certainly outweighed the low. In fact, she rarely expressed any regrets concerning her show business career, which spanned forty-five years. So it is ironic then that her last acting role ended sourly. After playing Miss Ellie on the long-running nighttime serial "Dallas," for one season, Donna was unceremoniously fired by the producers, who wanted to bring back Barbara Bel Geddes, the actress who originated the role. Donna was hurt and refused to be taken advantage of. A much publicized legal battle ensued, and Donna eventually won the lawsuit, but lost her fight to regain the role.

Shortly after her battle with "Dallas" ended, a more difficult one began. Donna was diagnosed with pancreatic cancer a few days before Christmas, 1985. Though her health seemed to be improving, she died on January 14, 1986.

It is sad that Donna's last dealings with the entertainment industry were so sour, and that "Miss Ellie" was to be her last role. Throughout her career, she had often expressed harsh opinions about Hollywood, the film industry, and male studio bosses. Far from being a difficult person, she was rather a strong-willed, opinionated individual, ready to stand up for her rights and unwilling to compromise her standards.

The unkind media headlines during the "Dallas" ordeal were most upsetting because they showed a lack of respect for an accomplished actress and a classy, dignified woman. Her forty films and early television work which have endured through time will hopefully overshadow any later unpleasant episodes in her career. Donna Reed deserves to be remembered as she was: an extraordinarily beautiful, intelligent, determined and talented woman, committed to her family and her career.

From Iowa farm girl to Academy Award winning actress, mother of four and "mother" to a nation of viewers, Donna Reed truly led a wonderful life.

It is the hope of the author that this book serve as a self-contained comprehensive research guide to the multi-faceted career of Donna Reed. Any suggestions for additions or corrections for future editions of this book are welcomed and can be sent to me in care of Greenwood Press.

Acknowledgments

I would like to express my sincerest gratitude to the
following individuals and organizations for their
assistance: research assistants Gary Crane and Lanette Hohl
and proofreader Lauren Royce Dickerson; Marilyn Herring and
Linda Kay for helping to locate articles; Jim Davidson for
much needed and appreciated help putting together my Episode
Guide; Art Pierce, Jay Hickerson and Ray Stanich for obscure
information on Donna Reed's radio career; Vicki Linde for
videotaping assistance; Katharine Loughney, Madeline Katz
and Edwin M. Matthias of the Motion Picture Department of
the Library of Congress; the Donna Reed Foundation for the
Performing Arts; the Lincoln Center Library for the
Performing Arts in New York, and the Academy of Motion
Picture Arts & Sciences Library in Los Angeles; The
Wisconsin Center for Film and Theater Research; Sandy Haynes
and the Norelius Community Library in Denison, Iowa; the
Movie/Entertainment Book Club; Jay Fultz, author of an
upcoming authorized Donna Reed biography, for sharing much
of his research and discoveries, and Grover Asmus for
granting his approval for my research.

For their support and encouragement, special thanks to
my family and friends.

Finally, thanks to James Robert Parish, series
adviser, and Marilyn Brownstein, humanities editor of
Greenwood Press for allowing me this opportunity.

Donna Reed

Biography

Donna Reed was born Donna Belle Mullenger, January 27, 1921, in Denison, Iowa. The oldest of William and Hazel Mullenger's five children, she was raised on her parents 140-acre farm approximately seven miles outside of Denison. Donna was a typical farm girl, who milked cows, and kept horses and ponies. She also looked after her younger brothers Keith and Billy, and younger sister Lavonne. (Another sister, Karen, was born after Donna left home). Her father was a farmer, her mother a teacher. One of Donna's favorite activities was going into town on Saturday nights-- the only time she saw anyone but her family through the week.

During grade school, Donna attended a one-room country school, Nishabotany No. 3, which had a total enrollment of twelve. At age thirteen, when it came time to transfer to high school, she moved in with her grandmother, Mrs. Mary Mullenger, in Denison-- a city of 4,000. The change was somewhat intimidating for the shy teenager, who hated large crowds of people. One of her teachers, Dr. Edward Tompkins, was instrumental in bringing her out of her shell (see B22, T6). He suggested she read "How to Win Friends and Influence People," and that she go out for dramatics. She followed his advice and gradually became popular. In her senior year she played the lead in the school play, The Night of January 16th, and was elected Campus Queen.

After graduating from Denison High School, Donna's ambitions included doing secretarial work and becoming a school teacher. Her initial goal, in any event, was to get a solid education. Unfortunately for Donna, these were the years of the Depression. The farm was suffering, and the family had been hit with hard times. A university education was not possible for Donna, but she didn't give up her plans. An aunt who lived in California wrote to Donna that the Los Angeles City College was offering good business courses for a low tuition. Donna reasoned that once she had a business education, she could work as a secretary until she had saved enough to go back to school for a degree in education.

These were Donna Mullenger's plans when the pretty seventeen-year-old arrived in Los Angeles in September of 1938. According to early articles written about her, she arrived with $60 in cash, driving a 1932 Ford sedan. She lived with her aunt, Mrs. Charles Von Rampen in South Gate, California while going to school and working part-time jobs to pay for books and tuition. When the distance between her aunt's and the college became unmanageable, she moved in with Mr. and Mrs. George Johnson, whom she regarded as family. She helped to cook and clean in exchange for room and board.

Living in Los Angeles, the home of the movie industry, Donna may have entertained notions of becoming a star. But even if she did, she never let herself stray from her prearranged plan. She worked hard to achieve the goals she set for herself, and proof of her levelheadedness came during her second year at school. On December 1st of that year she was again elected Campus Queen, this time of Los Angeles City College. The day after she was so named, her photo appeared in the Los Angeles Times and other local papers. By nightfall, as the story goes, she had received calls from several agents and movie studios.

Though she had appeared in two plays, The Intruder and The Happy Journey at L.A. City College, Donna had never thought seriously about becoming an actress, but with these offers she began to. She signed with the Feldman Bloom Agency, which handled Clark Gable and Claudette Colbert, but refused to consider any studio offers, determined to finish her education first. She was leery about the movie business and wanted a diploma more than she wanted a film contract. She even remained in school a month after her February 1941 graduation to study Private Speech and to brush up on her dramatic technique.

"It was like this-- If the movie idea didn't pan out, I wanted to have my shorthand to fall back on. After all, that's what I'd driven to Los Angeles for."[1]

Once she completed her business education, Donna relented, and an appointment was set for her first screen test, at Metro-Goldwyn-Mayer. She had been approached by three studios for screen tests and accepted the offer from MGM because it was the only movie company she had ever heard of (see B66). She tested with Van Heflin, an already established Broadway star. They were each signed to long-term contracts and given roles in an MGM production, The Get-Away (see F1). The studio's first order of business with their new ingenue was to change her name. Studio executives couldn't see Donna Mullenger on a theater marquis, so she promptly became Donna Adams.

As Donna Adams, she went to work in The Get-Away playing the heroine, opposite Robert Sterling. This Donna Adams' movie career was short-lived, however, when the studio heard of another actress named Donna Adams. The next name considered was Donna Drake, but someone recalled an actress named Dona Drake. One early article published in Donna's hometown newspaper reported that the name Donna Denison was being considered (see B20). It was probably MGM casting director Billy Grady who finally chose Donna Reed-- a name the actress never particularly liked.

"I hear 'Donna Reed' and I get a picture of a tall,
chic, austere blonde, which isn't me.   I've *never*
liked that name.   It has a cold, forbidding sound.
Donna Reed."[2]

Certainly Grady had a different image of the name, as
he recalls his first impression of the actress as being
anything but austere:
"I remember this beautiful, wide-eyed, frightened
child walking into my office.   I was struck by her
look of-- quality.   Please underline that 89 times:
quality."[3]

With her $75-a-week Metro contract, Donna moved from
the Johnson's into the Hollywood Studio Club on Lodi Place.
Living on a farm during the Depression had left its mark on
the young actress, who wouldn't take success for granted.
She practiced her shorthand regularly, just in case, and
looked at her acting as a job, in which intelligence and
hard work were key ingredients.
"I just knew that I wished to earn my living by
working for it.   I expected to do it in business, and
that's the way I'm looking at my job now.   I've had
to study and work, just the same, perhaps more than I
would have done as a secretary.   At least I'm not
going to start with any illusions that it's just
play."[4]

When <u>The Get-Away</u> opened in the summer of 1941 to
mixed reviews, twenty-year-old Donna was already at work on
<u>Shadow of the Thin Man</u>. By year's end, the busy actress had
completed her first four films for MGM.
Back on the farm the family was quite proud of Donna,
and the town of Denison celebrated "Mullenger Day" in the
movie star's honor (see B18). Movie magazines played up her
Iowa background in their pieces and more than one headline
called her the "farmer's daughter," prompting this quote in
a mid-1940s interview: "Please don't call me the 'farmer's
daughter' again.   I'm proud of the fact that I was born on a
farm, but I'm sure people are tired of hearing about it."
Family was always very important to Donna.   Her
salary as an actress allowed Donna to visit the farm more
frequently, and she kept in close touch with her family. As
the five Mullenger children grew and moved it became more
difficult to unite the entire family at once. Oldest
brother Keith moved to New York City and became an engineer.
Sister Lavonne moved to California and enjoyed a successful
modeling career, adopting "Heidi" as her professional name
(see R6). Brother Bill and sister Karen remained in Denison,
Bill running the farm. It took a 1958 "This is Your Life"
tribute to Donna to bring all five siblings and their
parents together at once, the first time in sixteen years
(see T6).
Lieutenant Jack Nau, a schoolmate of Donna's from
Denison, was frequently mentioned during this time in
magazine and newspaper items as her steady beau. He was an
Army flier stationed in Bakersfield, and they saw each other
occasionally.   However, a more serious relationship was
developing between Donna and an MGM makeup artist named Bill
Tuttle.   Reportedly, Bill had admired Donna since he first

saw her photo as Campus Queen, and paid special attention to her when she arrived at MGM.   They   met on   the set   of The Get-Away.

On January   30, 1943 Donna and William J. Tuttle were married at the Community Methodist Church   in Beverly Hills. Their   marriage   and   the   wedding   itself   received   little publicity, but their divorce two years   later did.   By that time,   Donna's   career   was   thriving,   and Louella Parsons, among others, reported on   their separation: "Neither Bill nor Donna   is talking   except to   say that   there is nothing they can explain beyond   the fact   that their...marriage has gone on the rocks."⁵

Donna didn't   talk much   about her   first marriage in later interviews either.   One rare reference to the marriage was made by her in a 1985 "Parade Magazine" interview.

> "Twenty-five   minutes   on   the   first   marriage   and twenty-five   years   on   the   next.   Ending   a short marriage is   not so   painful.   When you end one after 25   years,   it's   the   worst."⁶   (Reprinted   with permission from Parade, copyright © 1985.)

The second   marriage Donna   referred to   in the quote above was to Tony Owen, whom   she married   in June   of 1945, six months   after she divorced Tuttle.   Owen was working for Donna's agent, Charles K. Feldman, when they met.   He later said that   after he   took one look   at the   actress he decided he was   going to   marry her.   She   didn't like   Tony at the start and   thought nothing   of his   repeated advances.   They fought like cats and dogs while he was her agent (see B95). After her divorce they began dating, even though the gravel-voiced, opinionated agent   seemed   her   exact   opposite. She persisted in   calling   him   "Mr.   Owen"   probably up to the moment he popped the question (see B18).

The two were   married on June 15, 1945   at the Beverly Hills Community Church.   Donna wore navy blue gabardine with white hat and accessories.   Her sister Lavonne (Heidi) acted as maid   of honor.   Judy   Garland and   Vincent Minelli were married on the same day.   Louis B.   Mayer, head   of MGM, the studio where   both actresses   worked,   reportedly rushed from one wedding to the   other.   Both couples   then left   on the same train   toward their   honeymoon destinations.   Donna and Tony visited her family in Denison (see B22).

During this early part   of Donna's   career,   MGM was keeping her   busy with   a string of   supporting roles, including installments in three   of   their   low-budget, high profit   series.   (Shadow of   the   Thin   Man,   Calling Dr. Gillespie and   Courtship of   Andy Hardy.)   She   kept up her pace of four to five films a year during her first few years at the studio.   Her roles were generally undemanding, sweet-girl types for which she received little critical attention.

In 1945, Donna appeared on screen in only   two films, but her   screen presence   was being   taken more seriously by critics and moviegoers.   In The Picture of Dorian Gray, the film adaptation of Oscar   Wilde's classic novel, she played Dorian Gray's fiancée, a character added to the film to give it a romantic angle.   Next she garnered rave reviews for her work in They Were   Expendable with   John   Wayne   and Robert Montgomery.

Donna's nineteenth film was the first to take her off the Metro lot.   She   was   loaned   out   to   Frank   Capra at RKO/Liberty Films   for   It's   a Wonderful   Life   in 1946.   The film was a failure at the   box office   but has   since turned into   a   perennial   favorite, airing on television countless times during the Christmas season.   Donna Reed immortalized the role   of Mary Hatch, the beautiful adoring wife of Jimmy Stewart's George Bailey.

It is hard to imagine another actress in   the role of Mary, but Donna Reed was not the only one considered.   Capra first approached Jean Arthur for the   role, but   she refused due to   a prior commitment.   Capra's notes show that he also considered Olivia de Havilland, Martha Scott and Ann Dvorak. Gossip columnist Hedda Hopper had been reporting that Ginger Rogers   was   being   considered,   but   Capra's   files   do not indicate that she was ever sent a script.

"In fact   on March   15, two days after Hopper's story appeared, he signed fresh-faced Donna   Reed   for the part, and   records indicate   that he   had made up his mind to borrow her from MGM   as early   as January 30. Reed wanted the part, but Metro held out, refusing to lend her to Capra unless she signed a   new seven-year contract with MGM.   Since she had nearly two years to go on her current   one, she   was naturally reluctant. But by March 15 the deal was made, and Reed was asked to report the   following   week   for   her   costume and makeup tests."⁷

The   film   was   the   first   post-war project for both Capra and Jimmy Stewart,   and   Donna   remembers   it   being a particularly tense   set.   Concerned that the two men didn't think she could handle   the role,   she later   learned it was themselves   they   were   worried about, trying to reestablish their careers.

In later interviews, Donna   called   It's   a Wonderful Life   her   favorite   film.   It also remains Jimmy Stewart's favorite, and Frank Capra,   in   his   autobiography   The Name Above the   Title,   stated   "I   thought it was the greatest film I ever made.   Better yet, I thought it was the greatest film anybody ever made."⁸

The public reaction at the time of the film's release was   not   so   favorable.   Reviewers   were   kind,   but   not overenthusiastic, and the film floundered at the box office. The critics were impressed with Donna Reed however,   and the publicity campaign   surrounding   It's a Wonderful Life   helped to establish Donna as a major film personality.

It's a Wonderful Life, her first   film away   from the home lot,   proved a   learning experience   for Donna.   MGM, a studio   known   for   churning   out   glamorous,   star-studded productions light   on drama and void of any controversy, had provided Donna   with   a   foot   in   the   door   of   the movie industry.   But   she   soon   found   that   if she wanted more substantial roles she would have to try another studio.

"I was at Metro eight years.   When   they were stumped with me   they did one of three things: they put me in a 'B,' they loaned me out, or they let me sit."⁹

After   It's a Wonderful Life,   Donna expected MGM to be cooking up wonderful projects for her to follow up with.   To the contrary, the studio seemed to be at   a loss   of what to do with her and after one more film for the studio, Green Dolphin Street, she sat out the remainder of her contract.

In 1946, following her work on It's a Wonderful Life, Donna stepped into another new role-- that of mother. She and husband Tony Owen adopted a daughter, whom they named Penny Jane. Tony's longtime friend Randolph Scott suggested Penny, and Jane was Donna's grandmother. The following year they adopted a son, Tony Jr. Donna and Tony had believed they could not have any children of their own, due to an injury Owen sustained in the war. In July of 1949 they proved the doctors wrong, and Donna gave birth to a son, Timothy Grant Owen. "I always assumed, no matter what the doctors said, that I would have children. And I did. It worked out just fine."[10]

Donna's next two films, Beyond Glory and Chicago Deadline, were for Paramount, and then she signed her second studio contract-- with Columbia Pictures. Her association with Columbia was brief and fraught with discord.

Her husband, Tony Owen, had been recruited by Columbia boss Harry Cohn as his executive assistant. It was an all-consuming job with long hours and an exhaustive pace. He left the post after a year and a half. Cohn's biographer claims that Owen quit when Donna issued the ultimatum, "You'll have to decide whom you are married to-- Harry Cohn or me."[11] After his employment with Columbia ended, Owen concentrated on a career producing films.

Since MGM had not provided Donna with a blockbuster hit during her eight years with the studio, Harry Cohn made it a personal challenge to one-up MGM president Louis B. Mayer and find the actress a star-making role. When Columbia bought the rights to James Jones' novel From Here to Eternity, Donna was Cohn's first choice to play the prostitute Lorene. Director Fred Zinnemann was not in favor, but after Donna filmed three tests for the role, and Cohn gave in on some of Zinnemann's other casting choices, the director relented and Donna was signed for the role.

Cohn's foresight proved correct, and From Here to Eternity was a breakthrough for Donna. A complete change from the sweet, superficial parts she was known for, the role called for wide emotional range and power. Donna delivered, and her performance earned her the accolades of reviewers and her peers. The Academy of Motion Picture Arts and Sciences, whose membership is comprised of professionals in the film industry, voted Donna Reed the Best Actress in a Supporting Role in a motion picture in 1953.

The awards were presented on March 25, 1954 at the RKO Pantages Theatre in Hollywood. Walter Brennan read the nominees: Grace Kelly for Mogambo, Geraldine Page for Hondo, Marjorie Rambeau for Torch Song, Donna Reed for From Here to Eternity and Thelma Ritter for Pickup on South Street. When she heard her name announced as the winner, Donna sprinted down the aisle.

"'It was a long walk, I didn't think I would make it,' she said at the podium. 'As wonderful as From Here to Eternity was, what's even more wonderful is "Eternity" to here.' She walked backstage, started crying, and was surprised when someone told her she had run to the stage. 'I ran? I don't believe it.'"[12]

Much to Donna's surprise, the man who brought her the
award-winning role of Lorene, Harry Cohn cast her   next in a
fifteen day "B" picture. She was astonished that Cohn could
expect her to follow From Here to Eternity with anything
less than a first-rate film.   She refused to do the part.
He then assigned her to Westerns (They Rode West, Three
Hours to Kill).

Donna could not understand Cohn's treatment of her.
It is suggested in King Cohn (see B259) that the mogul may
have felt the actress was not sufficiently grateful for his
generosity.   By the time the Oscar nominations were
announced, the situation had become desperate. Feeling that
her career would be in serious jeopardy if she stayed with
Columbia, she instructed her agent, "ask for my release;
this is a matter of life or death." Shortly after the Oscar
ceremony, Cohn granted Donna's wish and freed her from her
contract.

Donna returned to MGM for her next picture, The Last
Time I Saw Paris, but "only for a visit." She continued to
free-lance during the next year and in 1956, despite
previous misfortune with long-term studio contracts, she
signed with Universal Pictures. Her third experience as a
contract player was the most short-lived. She played leading
roles in two Universal releases, but was then offered only
supporting roles.   This time, Donna was after more than a
release from the contract.   She sued the studio for over
$70,000.   Universal countersued on the grounds that she
refused a role they offered her.   The suit was eventually
settled out of court for an undisclosed sum (see B130).

Following Backlash and The Benny Goodman Story for
Universal, Donna starred in Beyond Mombasa, for
Columbia/Hemisphere.   Her husband Tony Owen produced the
film, which was shot on location in East Africa. Beyond
Mombasa marked Donna and Tony's first collaboration
professionally.   It was the only film they would make
together.

The next year, Donna and Tony collaborated on another
project-- a daughter. The couple now had four children:
Penny, Tony Jr., Timothy and baby Mary Anne. The two oldest
children were adopted, but Donna saw to it that all her
children were treated alike.

"We didn't talk about the adoption publicly for years
and years...I got lots of flak about why we were
keeping it secret.   We said 'We're not keeping it
secret. We just don't think because of the high
visibility of our family, these 10 and 12 year olds
should have to pick up a paper, and every time
there's something printed about their mother, read
that they're adopted.   That's their business.' And
you know, no one said one word for years."[13]

In 1958, Donna took her last starring role in a
motion picture.   After The Whole Truth (see F39) for
Columbia Pictures, Donna left films to concentrate on
television. She cited the lack of good film roles for women
and a desire for financial security among the reasons she
decided to give TV a try.   She and Tony had formed Todon
Productions, and they now looked for a vehicle to produce
for Donna's television series debut. Todon was a combination
of their first names.

In developing a series for Donna to star in, Tony and Donna considered several different scenarios, including Donna as a single secretary, and Donna as a diplomat's wife. The final formula chosen was a basic family show centering on Donna's character-- a housewife.

"The Donna Reed Show" saw Donna playing Donna Stone, mother of two and wife of a pediatrician. The series premiered on September 24, 1958 on ABC. Initially, the outlook was grim for the series, which was up against Milton Berle on NBC. Early ratings were unimpressive, but the show gradually built a strong following and turned into a surprise hit.

Costarring in "The Donna Reed Show" were Carl Betz as Dr. Alex Stone, and Shelley Fabares and Paul Petersen as the couple's teenage children, Mary and Jeff. In 1963, a younger sibling was introduced to the household when eight-year-old orphan Trisha came to live with the Stones. Trisha was played by Patty Petersen, Paul Petersen's real-life sister. Later the same year, Shelley Fabares left the series to concentrate on films (she costarred in Girl Happy with Elvis) and a recording career. During the show's run, both Fabares and Paul Petersen had become teen recording stars. Fabares' "Johnny Angel" and Petersen's "My Dad" were both incorporated in episodes of "The Donna Reed Show."

Carl Betz played Donna's handsome and successful husband, Dr. Alex Stone, with appealing charm. Though the comedy format didn't allow him to stretch his acting muscles very much, he was indeed a magnificent actor, getting superior reviews for his stage work and subsequent TV series "Judd for the Defense." He had no illusions as to who was the star of "The Donna Reed Show."

"Donna and Tony are friends of mine... But I never kidded myself about the series. Basically, they wrote for Donna. I had maybe three episodes that were good for me."[14]

In addition to starring in the series, Donna was very much involved with its production. She approved the scripts, casting and other creative aspects, while Tony oversaw all of the financial details. Series starring women were scarce during that time, and it was doubly unusual for a woman star to be coproducer of her own series.

A surprising effect of "The Donna Reed Show" was that it established Donna Reed as the new symbol of American motherhood. A nation of viewers watched Donna Stone hold her household together, solve her children's problems, dish up delectable meals and maintain a happy marriage and they began to emulate her. Donna was slow to realize her position as America's favorite mother.

"I honestly didn't know that I was a role model. I couldn't have been more surprised when women would come up to me and say, 'I can't really manage things as well as you can.'"[15]

Whether Donna knew it or not, with "The Donna Reed Show" the Donna Reed legend was being formed. Her reputation as the "perfect mother" caused women's magazines to print her parenting advice and recipes, and Donna wrote a few articles herself on her approach to parenthood. As further proof of her impact on American mothers, the

American Mother's Committee, the founders of Mother's Day, awarded Donna with a special citation.

In addition to the Mother's Committee award, Donna was presented a Golden Globe, a Genii Award, the Hollywood Press Association's Golden Apple Award, and a special award from the Women's Auxiliary to the American Medical Association. One award which eluded Donna was the Emmy, the television industry's equivalent to the Oscar. Nominated for the award four times, she came away from each awards ceremony without the statuette. In a 1961 article, she stated her feelings regarding the Emmy: "I know I'll never get one. They don't vote awards for light comedy."[16]

Starring in a series and raising four children left Donna with little free time. She refused numerous offers for guest star spots on other shows, preferring to devote her time off the set to her family. During the show's eight-year run, Donna lent her acting talents to only one outside project, the 1960 motion picture *Pepe*.

Pepe was a star-studded production directed by George Sidney for Columbia Pictures. George Sidney directed Donna's original Hollywood screen test at MGM and cast her as an extra in *Thousands Cheer* in 1943. Sidney later recalled his first impression of Donna:

"Donna had-- a quiet kind of sex. To me, Donna suggested an intriguing combination-- ice and fire."[17]

In 1960, Donna and the director traded guest appearances. Donna performed a cameo in his *Pepe,* and George Sidney in turn appeared in an episode of "The Donna Reed Show." In the episode, entitled "The Stones Go to Hollywood," George Sidney, playing himself, offers the Stone family cameo roles in his motion picture: *Pepe*.

At the end of nearly every season of "The Donna Reed Show" there was speculation as to whether or not the series would continue. The concern was not due to ratings or sponsors (the show wasn't lacking either), but rather to its star's reluctance to renew her contract each year.

In 1966, after eight years and 274 episodes, "The Donna Reed Show" wrapped production. All conceivable plot lines in the Stone household had been played out, and all involved agreed it was time to bow out gracefully. The tired star went into retirement, and announced her intentions to rest, travel and devote time to her family. Owen, who had once been a part-owner of the Detroit Lions, planned to purchase a National Hockey League franchise. (The deal fell through.)

In addition to traveling extensively, Donna took up photography and got involved in politics. During the Vietnam War she became a peace activist and in 1967 cofounded Another Mother for Peace, a group of mothers seeking an end to American involvement in Vietnam. Their slogan "war is not healthy for children and other living things" became recognized nationwide. In the mid-seventies the group shifted its focus to protesting nuclear power. Donna also served on the Screen Actors Guild's board of directors.

The years following "The Donna Reed Show" brought about many changes in Donna's life. The most drastic of these changes was the end of her twenty-six year marriage to Tony Owen. Termed "the world's worst mismatch" from the beginning, the couple's differences had finally torn them apart. The marriage had been in trouble for quite some time, but they "stuck it out for the children."

> "Getting divorced was terrible, but it was also terrible being married. You have to decide which is worse. Nothing new really happened. He didn't change, and neither did I. It was always a difficult marriage. We were so different in temperament.... You get to the point where you say to yourself, 'Is this how I'm going to spend the rest of my life-- not doing any of the things I enjoy doing?' How about having to negotiate for every event?...Eventually I just decided it had to end."[18]

In June of 1971, they divorced. The couple divided over three million dollars in community property, and Owen agreed to pay child support for their daughter Mary Anne, who was then fourteen years old. (Owen died in May, 1984.)

Following her divorce, Donna was reluctant to date again. Things changed when she met Colonel Grover Asmus, an aide to General Omar Bradley. They met at a mutual friend's dinner party, and when they saw each other across a crowded room, it was instant attraction. Donna waved her hand to show that she wasn't wearing a wedding ring. A few days later, she got a call from a friend saying that General Bradley wanted to meet her, and a date was set for Donna to join the General and his wife at the races. Mrs. Bradley told Donna "By the way, a Colonel Asmus will pick you up." Donna later revealed "it was a pretty poor plot, but I played along." (see B188)

Donna became Donna Reed Asmus on August 30, 1974. Her children, and Asmus' two grown children from his first marriage were "wonderfully approving" about the match. Asmus had retired from the Army and became a petroleum engineer. The couple moved to Seattle, and later to Tulsa, Oklahoma as his assignments took him. They kept a house in Corona del Mar, California.

Throughout the years Donna remained close to her "Donna Reed Show" costars, and the group got together monthly for lunch. In the late seventies, they discussed the possibility of filming a "Donna Reed Show" reunion special. In July of 1977 they sold the concept to ABC. Paul Petersen, who focused on a writing career after the series ended, wrote the script. Their plans were halted when they learned that Carl Betz had inoperable lung cancer. He died in January of 1978. None of the others felt they could do a reunion without Betz, so the project was dropped.

Once Donna left the entertainment industry, she was in no hurry to return. Although she did not officially go into retirement, she could afford to be selective about the parts she would play. She was offered several roles during the years since her series ended, but found most of the parts offered her were passive, weak women not in control of their own lives. She preferred not to work than to take roles which she considered to portray a negative image of women. "I didn't work because I didn't get the kind of scripts I wanted. I didn't want to play helpless women and victim roles."[19]

During this time, Donna often expressed harsh opinions about Hollywood and the motion picture industry, particularly their treatment of women. An outspoken women's rights advocate, she denounced male directors and producers for the overabundance of "neurotic, sick, amoral" female characters in films and television, and the scarcity of secure, strong-willed career women.

In 1979, after twelve years of retirement, Donna accepted a role in a television movie, "The Best Place to Be." Donna's character, Sheila Callahan, was a refreshing change from other roles she had been offered. When her husband dies of a heart attack, Sheila is left alone with two rebellious teenagers and very little money. She starts over and rebuilds her life, proving herself a "genuine heroine." Her television comeback received poor reviews, and it would take another four years for Donna to accept another acting role.

In "Deadly Lessons", which aired on ABC in March of 1983, Donna played the headmistress of a girl's school where a string of murders take place. The next year, she filmed a two hour "Love Boat" special in which she was again teamed with Efrem Zimbalist, Jr., her costar from "The Best Place to Be."

If Donna was looking for a strong female character, she couldn't have handpicked a better one than that of Miss Ellie Ewing, the matriarch of the Ewing family of "Dallas." Miss Ellie, who can stand up to the most powerful man on television-- the nasty J.R. Ewing-- without batting an eyelash, is a solid, traditional, family-oriented woman. Barbara Bel Geddes, the original Miss Ellie, left the role in 1984 after heart surgery. When producers were considering how to continue the show without Bel Geddes, they decided that the Miss Ellie role was a central force in the show and should not be written out.

Recasting a television character is a precarious practice. Faithful viewers have a hard time accepting a sudden change in actors. The producers were discussing actresses in the same age range, when somebody mentioned Donna Reed. They immediately jumped into action-- tracking down Donna's agent and finding out if the actress was available. When she got the call from producer Philip Capice, Donna jumped at the offer. She and her husband had moved back to California permanently and she was ready to take the plunge back into series TV. Since Donna would be only one star among many in the "Dallas" cast, her schedule would be much lighter than in her "Donna Reed Show" days, affording her plenty of time to spend with her family.

Her first "Dallas" episode aired on November 9, 1984. When Miss Ellie returned from her honeymoon with her new husband Clayton Farlow, played by Howard Keel, she appeared in the form of Donna Reed. No explanation was made for Miss Ellie's sudden change in appearance-- it was hoped that viewers would simply accept the new actress. Donna anticipated the reluctance of viewers to accept her in the role, but was optimistic about her chances.

"Fans will be sad to see that Barbara is no longer on the show. But if they have a choice between having a Miss Ellie and not having a Miss Ellie, I hope they'll be happy to see me."[20]

Donna's characterization of Miss Ellie was different from Bel Geddes', as she did not set out to copy from her

predecessor, but to interpret the role her own way. The
result was a "classier, more elegant" Miss Ellie. She was
gaining the acceptance of viewers, and her bosses were
equally satisfied. Originally signed to a one year
contract, at the end of the first season the producers
renewed her option for two more years. "Dallas" ratings
remained as high as they were during Bel Geddes' tenure.
      This time of her life was particularly happy for
Donna. Her marriage was very fulfilling and in interviews
she gushed superlatives when asked about her relationship
with Asmus. Her professional rebirth was another factor in
her happiness. She was thrilled to be working again,
especially on a hit series in a role she loved. "I'm crazy
about the part and feel very comfortable. Miss Ellie is
just right for me."²¹
      What followed is a sad commentary on the cold,
impersonal entertainment industry. A forty-five year
veteran of film, television and radio, the award-winning
actress was pushed aside when Barbara Bel Geddes decided to
return to "Dallas." Donna and her husband were vacationing
in Europe when, on April 11, 1985, she got a call from her
agent informing her that she had been fired so that Bel
Geddes could reclaim the role. "I was in shock. Stunned."
      Lorimar, the production company which owns "Dallas,"
made their official announcement to the press four days
later. They had tried to persuade Donna to tell the press
that she had only taken the role temporarily, and was gladly
stepping aside for Bel Geddes. Donna refused to go along
with their lies. She could not understand their treatment
of her and was not about to step aside gracefully. Instead
she fought back. She sued Lorimar for breach of contract,
asking $7.5 million dollars in damages. She also filed an
injunction to halt production of all scenes involving the
Miss Ellie character.
      A superior court judge denied her the injunction on
June 18, 1985. She was thus unable to prevent Bel Geddes
from stepping back into the role. She was more successful
with her breach of contract suit against Lorimar. In August
she settled out of court with the production company and was
awarded $1.25 million dollars. She called the settlement
"very fair and quite generous." She was also freed from all
contractual responsibilities to Lorimar. She could take any
acting jobs while still collecting her "Dallas" salary. She
chose instead to travel with her husband.
      Shortly after the "Dallas" ordeal ended, Donna faced
a much more serious crisis. On December 10, 1985 she
entered Cedars-Sinai Medical Center in Beverly Hills with a
bleeding ulcer. Exploratory surgery revealed that Donna had
pancreatic cancer. The cancer was malignant, and there was
little that doctors could do.
      She was released from the hospital on Christmas Eve
to spend the holidays with her family. Her condition seemed
to be improving. She died in her Beverly Hills home at 9:17
a.m. on January 14, 1986. Her husband of twelve years,
Grover Asmus was at her side.
      Donna was buried at Westwood Memorial Cemetery and a
memorial service was held at the Presbyterian Church of
Beverly Hills. The family requested that in place of
flowers, donations be sent to the American Cancer Society.

In memorial articles her friends and coworkers remembered her fondly:

Jimmy Stewart: "I've had a lot of screen wives, but I will always rank Donna right up there at the top. She was a very, very special person." [22]

Frank Sinatra: "I can remember in the beginning when every guy, particularly myself, who saw her on screen had a crush on Donna. She was a lovely lady, gentle and kind." [23]

Paul Petersen: "She was a giving woman who was always there to share and to help. She taught me oh so many things." [24]

Perhaps the most fitting remembrance was made by the Donna Reed Foundation for the Performing Arts (see the Appendix), an organization founded in Denison shortly after her death. The foundation's literature states that they were established "to memorialize Donna Reed and the principles for which she stood: honesty, integrity and commitment to family, community and profession." No description has come closer to capturing the essence of Donna Reed.

NOTES

1. "Iowa Corn to Cinema Queen- Donna's Done It!" *The Milwaukee Journal*, January 18, 1942, p. 3.

2. "The Farmer's Daughter Who Went to Town," *TV Guide*, May 6, 1961, p. 12.

3. Ibid, p. 14.

4. "Iowa Corn."

5. Louella O. Parsons, "Donna Reed, Husband Part," *Los Angeles Herald-Examiner*, December 13, 1944.

6. Tom Seligson, "Everybody's Mom?" *Parade Magazine*, February 3, 1985, p. 5.

7. Jeanine Basinger, *The "It's a Wonderful Life" Book* (New York: Alfred A. Knopf, Inc., 1986), p. 9. Reprinted with permission.

8. Frank Capra, *The Name Above The Title* (New York: Macmillan Company, 1971), p. 383.

9. William H. Brownell, Jr., "The Way to 'Eternity,'" *New York Times*, April 25, 1954, p. X5.

10. Seligson, "Everybody's Mom?" p. 6.

11. Bob Thomas, King Cohn: The Life and Times of Harry Cohn (New York: G.P. Putnam's Sons, 1967), p. 210.

12. Mason Wiley et al., Inside Oscar: The Unofficial History of the Academy Awards (New York: Ballantine Books, a Division of Random House, Inc., 1986), p. 241. Reprinted with permission.

13. Seligson, "Everybody's Mom?" p. 6.

14. Tom Mackin, "Betz to Play Hot Lawyer," Newark Evening News, May 21, 1967.

15. Seligson, "Everybody's Mom?" p. 7.

16. Bob Lardine, "It's Still a Man's World," New York Sunday News, August 13, 1961, p. 7.

17. "The Farmer's Daughter Who Went to Town," TV Guide, May 6, 1961, p. 14.

18. Seligson, "Everybody's Mom?" p. 7.

19. Yardena Arar, "TV Star Donna Reed Dies of Cancer," L.A. Life, Daily News, January 15, 1986, p. 16.

20. Michelle Green et al., "As Dallas' New Miss Ellie, Donna Reed Trades in the Kitchen for a Home on the Range," People Magazine, November 19, 1984, p. 94.

21. Kay Gardella, "Offscreen With the New Miss Ellie," New York Daily News, July 12, 1984, p. 86.

22. Mitchell Fink, "Donna Reed's Friends Say Last Goodbyes to 'Classy Lady'," Los Angeles Herald-Examiner, January 18, 1986.

23. Michael Seiler, "Donna Reed, Oscar Winner and TV Star, Dies at 64," Los Angeles Times, January 15, 1986, p. 16.

24. Bruce R. Miller, "Remembering Donna," Sioux City Journal, June 8, 1986, p. E1.

Chronology

January 27, 1921	Donna Belle Mullenger born in Denison, Iowa.
September 1934	Donna transferred from one-room country school to Denison High School; moved in with grandmother in Denison.
September 1938	Donna moved from Denison to California to attend Los Angeles City College
December 1, 1940	Donna Mullenger elected "Campus Queen" at L.A. City College
December 2, 1940	Photo as "Campus Queen" appeared in newspapers, spotted by agents and studios.
February 1941	Graduated from Los Angeles City College; MGM screen test with Van Heflin.
April 1941	Donna Mullenger signed $75 a week contract with MGM. Name changed to Donna Adams, later to Reed.
June 1941	Donna's first film, "The Get-Away" (MGM) opened to mixed reviews.
1941	"Shadow of the Thin Man" (MGM) "Babes on Broadway" (MGM) "The Bugle Sounds" (MGM)
1942	"Courtship of Andy Hardy" (MGM) "Mokey" (MGM) "Calling Dr. Gillespie" (MGM) "Apache Trail" (MGM) "Eyes in the Night" (MGM)

January 30, 1943

Married   MGM   make-up   artist William Tuttle.

1943

"Human Comedy" (MGM)
"Dr. Gillespie's Criminal Case" (MGM)
"Man from Down Under" (MGM)
"Thousands Cheer" (MGM)

1944

"See Here, Pvt. Hargrove" (MGM)
"Gentle Annie" (MGM)

January 1945

Divorced William Tuttle.

1945

"Picture of Dorian Gray" (MGM)
"They Were Expendable" (MGM)

June 15, 1945

Married agent Tony Owen.

1946

Donna and Tony Owen adopted first daughter, Penny Jane.

1946

"Faithful in my Fashion" (MGM)

March 15, 1946

Signed for role of Mary Hatch Bailey in "It's A Wonderful Life" (RKO/Liberty Films)

April 8, 1946

Shooting   began   on   "It's   A Wonderful Life."

December 1946

"It's a Wonderful Life" opened; a box office failure

1947

Donna and Tony Owen adopted a son, named Tony Jr.

1947

"Green Dolphin Street" (MGM)

April 1948

Her seven year contract up, Donna left Metro-Goldwyn-Mayer.

1948

"Beyond Glory" (Paramount)

July 1949

Donna gives birth to son, Timothy Grant Owen.

1949

"Chicago Deadline" (Paramount)

1950

Signed   contract   with   Columbia Pictures.

1951

"Saturday's Hero" (Columbia)

1952

"Scandal Sheet" (Columbia)
"Hangman's Knot" (Columbia)

1953

"Trouble Along the Way" (WB)
"Raiders of the Seven Seas" (UA)
"From Here to Eternity"(Columbia)

1953	"The Caddy" (Paramount) "Gun Fury" (Columbia)
February 15, 1954	Motion Picture Academy of Arts & Sciences announced the 1953 Academy Award nominees. Donna Reed was nominated for Best Supporting Actress.
March 25, 1954	Won Academy Award for "From Here to Eternity"
1954	"Three Hours to Kill" (Columbia) "They Rode West" (Columbia) "Last Time I Saw Paris" (MGM)
1954	Released from her contract with Columbia upon her request.
1955	"The Far Horizons" (Paramount)
March 30, 1955	Presented Academy Award to Edmond O'Brien for "The Barefoot Contessa" at the 1954 Academy Awards ceremony.
1956	"Ransom" (MGM)
1956	Signed contract with Universal. "The Benny Goodman Story" (Univ.) "Backlash" (Univ.)
1956	Ended association with Universal when they only offered her supporting roles.
1956	"Beyond Mombasa" (Columbia)
August 1956	Formed Todon Productions with husband Tony Owen.
May 1957	Daughter Mary Anne born.
1958	"The Whole Truth" (Columbia)
September 24, 1958	"The Donna Reed Show" premiered.
1960	Filmed a cameo role in "Pepe" (Columbia), her last film.
December 23, 1965	Last episode of "The Donna Reed Show" taped.
1967	Joined Another Mother For Peace.
June 10, 1971	Divorced Tony Owen.
August 30, 1974	Married Grover Asmus, retired U.S. Army colonel.

May 1979	TV Movie "The Best Place to Be" marked Donna's return to acting after a 13 year retirement.
June 1984	Took over the role of Miss Ellie on "Dallas."
November 9, 1984	Donna's first "Dallas" episode aired.
April 11, 1985	Fired by "Dallas" producers.
June 18, 1985	Lost legal fight to halt production of "Dallas."
August 1985	Settled lawsuit with "Dallas" producers for $1.25 million dollars
December 1985	Diagnosed with pancreatic cancer.
January 14, 1986	Died in Los Angeles, at age 64.
June 14, 1986	First annual Donna Reed Film Festival held in Denison, Iowa. Donna's Oscar was presented to the Crawford County Historical Society.

Donna Reed and Jimmy Stewart in a scene from the Christmas classic *It's a Wonderful Life* (1946).

Donna won an Academy Award for her portrayal of the "hostess" Lorene in *From Here to Eternity* (1953).

Gun-slinging Donna in a publicity shot for *Gun Fury* (1953).

Donna received outstanding reviews for her portrayal of the legendary Indian guide Sacajawea in *The Far Horizons* (1955).

Filmography

For each of Donna Reed's forty film appearances, individual film reviews are listed following the film synopsis. Where sufficient information or anecdotes regarding that film can be found in other sources listed in the Bibliography, those articles are cross-referenced following the reviews.

F1.   *THE GET-AWAY*   (88 min., B/W)

Metro-Goldwyn-Mayer, 1941
Producer: J. Walter Ruben
Director: Edward Buzzell
Screenplay: Wells Root and W.R. Burnett
Based on a story by: J. Walter Ruben and Wells Root

Cast: Robert Sterling (*Jeff Crane*), Charles Winninger (*Dr. Josiah Glass*), Donna Reed (*Maria Theresa O'Reilly*), Henry O'Neill (*Warden Alcott*), Dan Dailey Jr. (*Sonny Black*), Don Douglas (*Jiff Duff*), Ernest Whitman (*"Moose"*), Grant Withers (*Parker*)

Synopsis: Jeff Crane is an FBI agent who goes undercover as a prisoner. He shares a cell with big time gangster Sonny Black, whose gang the FBI wants to round up. As part of the FBI's plot, Crane organizes a prison break for himself and Black, and once outside he infiltrates the gang. When Crane falls for Black's beautiful sister, he is discredited by his chief. The entire gang is gunned down by Federal agents in an exciting finale.

Review excerpts: According to <u>Variety</u> (6/18/41), the film has "plenty of suspense and excitement" and in her first film appearance, Donna Reed "displays poise, ability and personality."

The film received a less than favorable review from Bosley Crowther of the <u>New York Times</u> (7/17/41, p. 23), who called it "routine fiction in the cops-and-robbers vein." This brief review does not comment on Donna's performance.

F2.   *SHADOW OF THE THIN MAN*   (97 min., B/W)

Metro-Goldwyn-Mayer, 1941
Producer: Hunt Stromberg
Director: Major W.S. Van Dyke II
Screenplay: Irving Brecher and Harry Kurnitz
Story by: Harry Kurnitz
Based on characters created by: Dashiell Hammett

Cast: William Powell (*Nick Charles*), Myrna Loy (*Nora Charles*), Barry Nelson (*Paul Clarke*), Donna Reed (*Molly Ford*), Sam Levene (*Lt. Abrams*), Alan Baxter (*Whitey Barrow*), Dickie Hall (*Nick Charles, Jr.*), Loring Smith (*Link Stephens*), Stella Adler (*Claire Porter*), Lou Lubin (*Rainbow Benny*), Louise Beavers (*Stella*) and Asta.

Synopsis: Nick and Nora Charles are visiting the track when a jockey is murdered. Later a reporter is murdered and Nick can no longer resist investigating. When Nick deduces that the jockey's death was the result of a bizarre accident, he doesn't let on to the press- but leads them instead to believe that the same person committed both murders. As expected, the real murderer tries to frame someone for the jockey's death in order to get himself off the hook, and Nick neatly wraps up the case. Donna Reed plays Molly Ford, whose boyfriend is one of the prime suspects.

Reviews: The critic for <u>Variety</u> (10/22/41) gave the film a very favorable review, citing "a lively script, spirited dialog and amusing situations." Though Donna isn't mentioned individually in the text of the review, it states that the supporting roles are performed by "capable players."

Theodore Strauss, for the <u>New York Times</u> (11/21/41), felt that the film was not up to the quality of earlier "Thin Man" entries, but that it has some "exciting moments." Donna's performance is not mentioned.

Additional reviews: <u>Commonweal</u>, 11/28/41, p. 144; <u>Newsweek</u>, 11/24/41, p. 73, <u>Time</u>, 12/8/41, p. 97

F3.   *BABES ON BROADWAY*   (121 min., B/W)

Metro-Goldwyn-Mayer, 1941
Producer: Arthur Freed
Director: Busby Berkeley
Screenplay by: Fred Finklehoffe, Elaine Ryan
Based on a story by: Burton Lane

Cast: Mickey Rooney (*Tommy Williams*), Judy Garland (*Penny Morris*), Fay Bainter (*Miss Jones*), Virginia Weidler (*Barbara Jo*), Ray MacDonald (*Ray Lambert*), Richard Quine (*Morton Hammond*), Donald Meek (*Mr. Stone*), Alexander Woollcott (*Himself*), Luis Alberni (*Nick*), Donna Reed (*Secretary*), Joe Yule (*Mason, Aide to Reed*)

Synopsis: This sequel to Babes In Arms has Mickey Rooney and Judy Garland leading a group of youngsters trying to break into show business. They stage a settlement house show in order to raise money to help some underprivileged kids. Mainly a vehicle for Rooney to sing, dance and do impressions.

Reviews: Reviewers singled out Mickey Rooney's performance as the highlight of this film. The New York Times (1/1/42, p. 37) reviewer called the production "dull and overly long," while Variety's more encouraging review (12/3/41) listed the "stupendous minstrel show" and "production numbers on an elaborate scale" among the film's assets. Donna's role in this film is small, and she is not mentioned in the reviews.

Additional reviews: Commonweal, 1/9/42, p. 296; Newsweek, 1/5/42, p. 54; Scholastic, 1/5/42, p. 32; Time, 1/19/42, p. 32

F4.   *THE BUGLE SOUNDS*   (101 min., B/W)

Metro-Goldwyn-Mayer, 1941
Producer: J. Walter Ruben
Director: S. Sylvan Simon
Screenplay: Cyril Hume
Based on a story by: Lawrence Kimble and Cyril Hume

Cast: Wallace Beery (*Hap Doan*), Marjorie Main (*Susie*), Lewis Stone (*Col. Lawton*), George Bancroft (*Russell*), William Lundigan (*Joe Hanson*), Henry O'Neill (*Lt. Col. Seton*), Donna Reed (*Sally Hanson*), Roman Bohnen (*Leech*), Guinn 'Big Boy' Williams (*Krims*), Ernest Whitman (*Cartaret*)

Synopsis: An old Cavalry Sergeant rebels against the "mechanization" of the Army. He bitterly protests as his beloved horse is replaced by new-fangled, streamlined tanks. Suspected of sabotage, he is discharged for his insubordination. He bails the cavalry out of trouble and is reinstated in the finale. Beery plays the Sergeant, with Marjorie Main as his down to earth girlfriend, and Donna Reed and William Lundigan as a young married couple.

Review excerpts: A film "packed with sound patriotic fervor, thrills and comedy... heightened by excellent performances by the stars and balance of the cast" was how Variety (12/17/41) appraised The Bugle Sounds.

Bosley Crowther of the New York Times (4/3/42, p. 25) was less impressed by this "wholly unglamorous" Wallace Beery vehicle whose story "makes for situations more than sense."

Additional Reviews: Commonweal, 5/27/42, p. 562

F5.   *THE COURTSHIP OF ANDY HARDY*   (94 min., B/W)

Metro-Goldwyn-Mayer, 1942
Producer: Carey Wilson
Director: George B. Seitz
Screenplay: Agnes Christine Johnson
Based on characters created by: Aurania Rouverol

Cast: Mickey Rooney (*Andy Hardy*), Lewis Stone (*Judge Hardy*), Cecilia Parker (*Marian Hardy*), Fay Holden (*Mrs. Emily Hardy*), Steve Cornell (*Stewart Dwight*), Ann Rutherford (*Polly Benedict*), Sara Haden (*Aunt Milly*), Donna Reed (*Melodie Nesbit*), William Lundigan (*Jeff Willis*), Frieda Inescort (*Mrs. Nesbit*), Harvey Stephens (*Mr. Nesbit*), Betty Wells (*Susie*), Joseph Crehan (*Peter Dugan*)

Synopsis: Donna Reed plays Melodie Nesbit, a plain Jane who is brought out of her shell by Andy, who dates her as a favor to his father. Judge Hardy presided over the girl's parents' divorce trial and is worried about what their feuding is doing to the young girl, who seems unusually shy and withdrawn. Concurrently, Andy gets himself into some legal trouble by accidentally stealing a car. When he goes to his father for help, the judge decides to trade favors with Andy, and Andy asks Melodie out on a date. Melodie develops quite a crush on Andy, but Andy doesn't seem to return her feelings and even puts her down when he's with his friends. Her transformation from a shy frump to the stunning belle of the ball doesn't even open Andy's eyes. As wise Judge Hardy predicts, once Melodie's family situation improves, she no longer needs Andy, and easily recovers from her broken heart.

Reviews: Bosley Crowther, for the New York Times (4/10/42) called this twelfth film in the series "one of the less distinguished Hardy films." The review is unflattering overall, but singles out Donna Reed, "who plays the new girl....for she has looks and grace and a most appealing charm. Andy should keep in touch with her; he could go far and do a lot worse."

Variety's flattering review (2/11/42) called the film "solid entertainment...studded with laugh lines" and praised the cast entire cast and director Seitz.

See also: Donna's obituary in the Los Angeles Times (B218) claims that she complained to Louis B. Mayer about her frumpy role.

The Nine Lives of Mickey Rooney by Arthur Marx, (New York: Stein & Day, 1986, p. 113) contains an anecdote about the casting of the role of Melodie, which Mickey Rooney tried to secure for his then wife, Ava Gardner. It is said that producer Carey Wilson chose Donna Reed over Ava because he wanted someone with more experience.

F6.   *MOKEY*   (88 min., B/W)

Metro-Goldwyn-Mayer, 1942
Producer: J. Walter Ruben
Director: Wells Root
Screenplay: Wells Root and Jan Fortune
Based on stories by: Jennie Harris Oliver

Cast: Dan Dailey Jr., (*Herbert Delano*), Donna Reed (*Anthea Delano*), Bobby 'Robert' Blake (*Mokey Delano*), William "Buckwheat" Thomas (*Brother Cumby*), Cordell Hickman (*Booker T. Cumby*), Etta McDaniel (*Cindy Molishus*), Marcella Moreland (*Begonia Cumby*)

Synopsis: When nine year old Mokey Delano's father remarries, the boy has a hard time dealing with his new stepmother. He runs away, and his disobedience nearly lands him in reform school.

Review excerpts: Variety (3/25/42) labeled the film "rambling" and "loosely-woven" in their unflattering review. From the same review: "Donna Reed is good as the new wife in the household who tried to understand the mischievousness of her newly-acquired stepson."

F7.   *CALLING DR. GILLESPIE*   (84 min., B/W)

Metro-Goldwyn-Mayer, 1942
Director: Harold S. Bucquet
Screenplay: Willis Golbeck & Harry Ruskin
Based on story by Kubec Glasmon
From characters created by: Max Brand

Cast: Lionel Barrymore (*Dr. Leonard Gillespie*), Philip Dorn (*Dr. John Hunter Gerniede*), Phil Brown (*Roy Todwell*), Donna Reed (*Marcia Bradburn*), Nat Pendleton (*Joe Wayman*), Mary Nash (*Emma Hope*), Alma Kruger (*Molly Byrd*), Walter Kingsford (*Dr. Walter Carew*), Nell Craig (*Nurse Parker*), Jonathan Hale (*Frank Todwell*)

Synopsis: A continuation of the Dr. Kildare film series, the focus shifted to Dr. Gillespie when Lew Ayres, the actor who played Kildare, declared conscientious objector status in World War II. Story begins when sixteen-year-old Marcia Bradburn is frightened by her fiance's erratic behavior and memory lapses and turns to Dr. Gillespie to cure him. The wheelchair ridden doctor in turn enlists the aid of Dr. Gerniede, a surgeon who would rather be practicing psychiatry. Dr. Gerniede observes Roy Todwell, and concludes that the young man is mentally unbalanced and potentially very dangerous. Dr. Gillespie also examines Todwell and comes to the same conclusion. The boy's parents do not believe Gillespie's claim that their son has homicidal tendencies, and they refuse to have him treated. Gillespie's interference turns Todwell against him, and the boy begins threatening the old doctor's life. Todwell commits a string of murders before breaking into Blair Hospital to kill Gillespie. He is stopped by Joe Wayman, Gillespie's unofficial bodyguard. In a tidy wrap-up, Todwell is arrested, Wayman promoted, Gerniede transferred to psychiatry, and Marcia Bradburn saved from marrying a homicidal maniac.

Review excerpts: This chapter in the Dr. Kildare series was termed "awkward" by Theodore Strauss of the New York Times (7/9/42, p. 17). Philip Dorn and Donna Reed are deemed "personable and capable newcomers."

In the estimation of the reviewer from Variety (6/17/42), Donna Reed "lends a decorative touch" to this "mild entry."

Note: Donna's character was one of several from this film carried over into "Dr. Gillespie's Criminal Case" (see F10).

F8.   *APACHE TRAIL*   (66 min., B/W)

Metro-Goldwyn-Mayer, 1942
Producer: Samuel Marx
Director: Richard Thorpe
Screenplay: Maurice Geraghty
Based on a story by: Ernest Haycox

Cast: Lloyd Nolan (*'Trigger' Bill Folliard*), Donna Reed (*Rosalia Martinez*), William Lundigan (*Tom Folliard*), Ann Ayars (*Constance Selden*), Connie Gilchrist (*Señora Martinez*), Chill Wills (*'Pike' Skelton*), Miles Mander (*James V. Thorne*), Gloria Holden (*Mrs. James V. Thorne*), Ray Teal (*Ed Cotton*), Grant Withers (*Lestrade*)

Synopsis: Tom Folliard takes over command of a stagecoach station in Apache territory. He runs the station successfully and wins the respect of all, especially young Rosalia Martinez. When Folliard's no-good brother 'Trigger' Bill shows up, trouble follows. The Apaches attack the station, but they will retreat if Tom hands his brother (who stole an Apache peace pipe) over to them. Tom doesn't turn his brother out and fights off the Indian attack.

Reviews: Variety (6/24/42) called the film "a moderately entertaining western" and claimed that the three stars "all acquit themselves well."

F9.   *EYES IN THE NIGHT*   (80 min., B/W)

Metro-Goldwyn-Mayer, 1942
Producer: Jack Chertok
Director: Fred Zinnemann
Screenplay: Guy Trosper, Howard Emmett Rodgers
Based on novel Odor of Violets by: Baynard Kendrick

Cast: Edward Arnold (*Capt. Duncan Maclain*), Ann
Harding (*Norma Lawry*), Donna Reed (*Barbara Lawry*),
Allen Jenkins (*Marty*), John Emery (*Paul Gerente*),
Horace McNally (*Gabriel Hoffman*) Katherine Emery
(*Cheli Scott*), Rosemary DeCamp (*Vera Hoffman*)

Synopsis: The central   character in this mystery is
Captain Maclain, a blind private investigator, who is
called in to investigate the murder of an actor.
Paul Gerente, the victim, was engaged to marry young
Barbara Lawry, and had at one time also been involved
with the girl's stepmother. Norma Lawry had tried to
prevent her stepdaughter from marrying Gerente, and
she was standing nearby when the actor's body was
discovered. For these reasons, Barbara believes from
the start that her stepmother is the murderer.
Further plot complications arise when Maclain
uncovers a group of Nazi spies out to steal a secret
war formula invented by the girl's father.

Review excerpts: Theodore Strauss, in his New York
Times (10/16/42, p. 23) review, called the film a
"tidy and tingling little thriller." He added that
"Ann Harding, Allen Jenkins and Donna Reed and a
smart 'seeing-eye' shepherd dog are all adequate to
their undemanding roles."

Variety's (9/9/42) reviewer complimented Donna Reed's
performance above and beyond anything else in the
film: "Outstanding is Donna Reed as Miss Harding's
wilful, precocious stepchild... Miss Reed clicks
photogenically and otherwise despite hackneyed
material."

Additional reviews: Commonweal, 10/30/42, p. 44;
Scholastic, 11/9/42, p. 35

F10.   *THE HUMAN COMEDY*   (117 min., B/W)

Metro-Goldwyn-Mayer, 1943
Producer: Clarence Brown
Director: Clarence Brown
Screenplay: Howard Eastabrook
Based on the novel by: William Saroyan

Cast: Mickey Rooney, (*Homer Macauley*), Frank Morgan
(*Willie Grogan*), James Craig (*Tom Spangler*), Marsha
Hunt (*Diana Steed*), Fay Bainter (*Mrs. Macauley*), Ray
Collins (*Mr. Macauley*), Van Johnson (*Marcus
Macauley*), Donna Reed (*Bess Macauley*), Jackie "Butch"
Jenkins (*Ulysses Macauley*), Dorothy Morris (*Mary

Arena), John Craven (*Tobey*), Mary Nash (*Miss Hicks*),
Carl "Alfafa" Switzer (*Auggie*)

Synopsis: Rooney plays Homer Macauley, a telegram
delivery boy in a small town during the war. The
story follows the entire Macauley family, and is
narrated by Collins, as the father, who speaks from
heaven as it is two years after his death. Oldest
brother Marcus is a soldier in the Army who talks and
thinks of nothing but getting back safely to his
family and girlfriend Mary. Sister Bess is the sweet
college student, helping to take care of the family.
Youngest brother Ulysses steals the show scene after
scene, and the film has some truly funny moments
despite its overall serious tone. Homer, in his job
as telegram boy, delivers many War Department notices
to families of those killed in action. The stress of
the job affects he and the older telegraph operator,
Mr. Grogan, until finally the tragedy of the
situation strikes home. The last message Grogan
receives before dying of a heart attack over his
telegraph machine is that Marcus Macauley was killed.
Homer, the man of the family now, must break the news
to the rest of the family.

Academy Awards: Best original story
Academy Award nominations: Best Picture, Best
Director, Best Cinematography, Best Actor (Rooney).

Reviews: Bosley Crowther's mixed review in The New
York Times (3/3/43) went from hot to cold as he
compared the "moments of extraordinary beauty" to
what he called the "stretches of sheer banality."

The Variety review on the same day was more
favorable, citing the "brilliant expositions of the
family" as part of the "dramatic magic" of the piece.

Donna's performance is not mentioned individually in
either of the above reviews, but excellent notices
are given to the cast in general with standouts
Mickey Rooney, Frank Morgan and Jack Jenkins getting
highest praises.

Additional reviews: Agee on Film, vol. 1, p. 30-33;
Commonweal, 3/19/43, p. 543; Film Daily, 3/1/43, p.
8; Hollywood Reporter, 2/26/43, p. 3; Magill's Survey
of Cinema II, v. 3, p. 1073; Newsweek, 3/15/43, p.
78; Time, 3/22/43, p. 56

F11.   *DR. GILLESPIE'S CRIMINAL CASE*   (89 min., B/W)

Metro-Goldwyn-Mayer, 1943
Director: Willis Goldbeck
Screenplay: Martin Berkeley, Harry Ruskin &
    Lawrence P. Bachmann
Based on characters created by: Max Brand
British title: Crazy to Kill

Cast: Lionel Barrymore (*Dr. Leonard Gillespie*), Van Johnson (*Dr. Randall Adams*), Donna Reed (*Marcia Bradburn*), Keye Luke (*Dr. Lee Wong How*), John Craven (*Roy Todwell*), Nat Pendleton (*Joe Wayman*), Alma Kruger (*Molly Byrd*), William Lundigan (*Alvin F. Peterson*), Margaret O'Brien (*Margaret*), Walter Kingsford (*Dr. Walter Carew*)

Synopsis: Psychopathic killer Roy Todwell is the object of Dr. Gillespie's efforts in this film. Gillespie is trying to get Todwell transferred from prison into a psychiatric hospital on the grounds that he is insane. Before he is able to arrange the transfer, Todwell is killed in a prison break. Other plot concerns are the testing of two interns for the position of Gillespie's assistant, and an epidemic outbreak among children.

Review excerpts: <u>Variety</u> (5/5/43): "The strain of keeping Dr. Gillespie alive as a screen character in a series that has extended over the years is beginning to tell- all hands concerned have failed to provide anything but mediocre screen entertainment." Donna is mentioned as a carryover in the series, but her performance is not commented on.

Note: Donna's character originated in the film <u>Calling Dr. Gillespie</u> (see F6), the previous installment in the Dr. Kildare/Dr Gillespie series.

F12. *THE MAN FROM DOWN UNDER* (103 min., B/W)

Metro-Goldwyn-Mayer, 1943
Producer: Robert Z. Leonard and Orville O. Dull
Director: Robert Z. Leonard
Screenplay: Wells Root and Thomas Seller
Based on a story by: Bogart Rogers and Mark Kelly

Cast: Charles Laughton (*Jocko Wilson*), Binnie Barnes (*Aggie Dawlins*), Richard Carlson (*'Nipper' Wilson*), Donna Reed (*Mary Wilson*), Christopher Severn (*Nipper as a child*), Clyde Cook (*Ginger Gaffney*), Horace McNally (*'Dusty' Rhodes*), Arthur Shields (*Father Polycarp*)

Synopsis: At the end of World War I, an Australian Sergeant adopts two young refugee children before returning home to Australia. He leaves the woman he was supposed to marry behind on the dock. As the years pass the boy becomes a championship boxer and the girl is sent to finishing school. Jocko Wilson becomes proprietor of a large hotel. Mary and Nipper, the now grown children raised by Wilson, find themselves falling in love with one another. Both are miserable, and Mary rejects advances made by an American reporter. Aggie Dawlins, the woman scorned by Wilson, turns up at the inn. She gains her revenge by gambling with Wilson and winning the hotel. World War II breaks out and the group is stuck together in the hotel, under threat of a Japanese attack. Under these conditions, Wilson and Dawlins reconcile, and it is finally revealed that Mary and Nipper are not really siblings and the pair are free to be together.

Review excerpts: Theodore Strauss remarked, "as the young lovers, Richard Carlson and Donna Reed, a capable and attractive actress, are quite helpless against a foolish situation" in his review for the New York Times (9/27/43, p. 23).

From Variety's review on 8/4/43, "both Carlson and Reed deliver top-notch performances" in this "refreshing screen tale."

Additional reviews: Cosmopolitan, 12/43, p. 96; New Yorker, 9/27/43, p. 23; Newsweek, 10/4/43, p. 107

F13.   *THOUSANDS CHEER*   (126 min., Color)

Metro-Goldwyn-Mayer, 1943
Producer: Joseph Pasternak
Director: George Sidney
Screenplay: Paul Jarrico and Richard Collins
Based on their story "Private Miss Jones"

Cast: Kathryn Grayson (*Kathryn Jones*), Gene Kelly (*Eddie Marsh*), Mary Astor (*Hyllary Jones*), John Boles (*Colonel Jones*), Ben Blue (*Chuck*), Frances Rafferty (*Marie*), Jose Iturbi (*Himself*), Dick Simmons (*Captain Avery*), and the "MGM Hit Parade" (Mickey Rooney, Judy Garland, Lionel Barrymore, Red Skelton, Lucille Ball, Ann Sothern, June Allyson, Donna Reed, Frank Morgan, Lena Horne, Margaret O'Brien, several others)

Synopsis: The plot of this star-studded MGM musical concerns the courtship of singer Kathryn Jones, daughter of the commandant at an Army base and Eddie Marsh, a private under her father's command. The plot however takes a backseat to the spectacular all-star variety show which Kathryn puts together to entertain the troops. MGM stars play themselves in skits and musical numbers. Mickey Rooney is the Master of Ceremonies and does hilarious impersonations of Clark Gable and Lionel Barrymore. Among the acts: Judy Garland sings "The Joint is Really Jumpin'" and Red Skelton does a skit in which he plays an ice cream parlor clerk. Donna Reed plays one of Skelton's customer's, a woman he can't recall having met before.

Review excerpts: Thomas M. Pryor of the New York Times (9/14/43, p. 27) called the film "two solid hours of magnificent entertainment."

Variety (9/15/43) concurred: "Metro has a smash in this all-star, technicolorful filmusical." Donna Reed is not mentioned in the reviews, as she only performed a brief cameo.

F14.   *SEE HERE, PRIVATE HARGROVE*   (102 min., B/W)

Metro-Goldwyn-Mayer, 1944
Producer: George Haight
Director: Wesley Ruggles, Tay Garnett (uncredited)
Screenplay: Harry Kurnitz
Based on the novel by: Marion Hargrove

Cast: Robert Walker (*Private Marion Hargrove*), Donna
Reed (*Carol Holliday*), Keenan Wynn (*Private
Mulvehill*), Robert Benchley (*Mr. Holliday*), Ray
Collins (*Brodie S. Griffith*), Chill Wills (*First
Sergeant Cramp*), Bob Crosby (*Bob*), Marta Linden (*Mrs.
Holliday*), Grant Mitchell (*Uncle George*), George
Offerman Jr. (*Private Esty*), Edward Fielding (*General
Dillon*), Donald Curtis (*Sergeant Heldon*)

Synopsis: Taken from the best-selling novel based on
the author's own military experience, See Here,
Private Hargrove is set in a peacetime U.S. Army
camp. Private Marion Hargrove begins as a reporter
whose ineptitude drives his editor crazy. He is then
drafted into the Army, where his blundering ways earn
him nearly continual K.P. duty. He meets Carol
Holliday, and just as the young couple are beginning
their romance, she moves to New York with her family.
Hargrove sells shares in his literary career to two
buddies to get money to visit her. His new found
love turns him into a letter perfect soldier, and he
even merits a temporary promotion. The remainder of
the plot concerns Hargrove and buddy Mulvehill's
wangling easy office posts while their pals are being
shipped into combat. Their consciences get the
better of them and they conspire to rejoin their unit
just before their train departs.

Review excerpts: Variety's reviewer (2/23/44, p. 10)
was unrestrained in his praise of Donna. "Donna Reed,
photographing like the proverbial million, is the
topper... Miss Reed registers stunningly for
appearance and delivery... She's missed when not in
action."

Bosley Crowther of the New York Times (3/22/44, p.
17) gave the film an excellent review calling it a
"joyous manifestation of fun and frolic." He adds
enigmatically, "...and Donna Reed is poetically
licensed as the girl whom he conveniently comes to
love."

Howard Barnes, New York Herald Tribune, 3/22/44:
"Donna Reed is attractively restrained as the girl."

Additional reviews: Commonweal, 3/17/44, p. 544;
Film Daily, 2/18/44, p. 6; Hollywood Reporter,
2/14/44, p. 3; Life, 3/27/44, p. 119-20; Newsweek,
3/6/44, p. 80; Photoplay, 3/44, p. 48-49; Time,
3/20/44, p. 94

F15.   *GENTLE ANNIE*   (80 min., B/W)

Metro-Goldwyn-Mayer, 1944
Producer: Robert Sisk
Director: Andrew Marton
Screenplay: Lawrence Hazard
Based on a novel by: Mackinlay Kantor

Cast: James Craig (*Lloyd Richland*), Donna Reed (*Mary Lingen*), Marjorie Main (*Annie Goss*), Henry Morgan (*Cottonwood Goss*), Paul Langton (*Violet Goss*), Barton MacLane (*Sheriff Tatum*), John Philliber (*Barrow*), Morris Ankrum (*Gansby*)

Synopsis: Pioneer woman Annie Goss and her two sons rob a train in order to migrate from Oklahoma to Missouri.   U.S. Marshall Lloyd Richland takes a liking to the three after they befriend him by letting him stay with them. Despite incriminating evidence, Richland believes in their innocence. Mary Lingen, a waitress who quit her job and is left stranded, also comes to stay with the family of robbers and becomes romantically involved with the Marshall. "Gentle" Annie and the boys are so likable that even after he discovers their guilt, the Marshall remains on their side. He lets the brothers escape when their mother is shot, and then allows them to get into a gunfight in which one of them is killed.

Review excerpts: Bosley Crowther of the New York Times (5/5/45, p. 11) declared "Gentle Annie" a "pleasantly sentimental film" with "a good bit of tender romance...nicely enacted by James Craig and Donna Reed."

Of Donna's performance, Variety (12/20/44) said "she's okay."

See also: B13 ("Go Western Young Lady"): Donna discusses her experiences filming Gentle Annie.

F16.   *THE PICTURE OF DORIAN GRAY*   (110 min., B/W-Color)

Metro-Goldwyn-Mayer, 1945
Producer: Pandro S. Berman
Director: Albert Lewin
Screenplay: Albert Lewin
Based upon the novel by: Oscar Wilde

Cast: George Sanders (*Lord Henry Wotton*), Hurd Hatfield (*Dorian Gray*), Donna Reed (*Gladys Hallward*), Angela Lansbury (*Sybil Vane*), Peter Lawford (*David Stone*), Lowell Gilmore (*Basil Hallward*), Richard Fraser (*James Vane*), Douglas Walton (*Allen Campbell*), Morton Lowry (*Adrian Singleton*)

Synopsis: This dramatization of Oscar Wilde's classic novel tells the story of Dorian Gray, a man

who remains mysteriously young through the years
while his portrait takes on all the signs of his age
and corruption. While viewing his picture, painted
by friend Basil Hallward, Gray's vanity and fear of
aging inspire him to make a pact, trading his soul
for eternal youth. From that point forward, Gray's
physical appearance never changes. He leads a life
full of implied evil, and each scandalous act
contributes to the hideous distortion of the
painting. Driven to madness in the end, he tries to
destroy the painting by plunging a knife into the
canvas. It is he who is destroyed, as the picture is
suddenly restored to its original condition and Gray
himself is transformed into the grotesque character
of the portrait. The knife plunged through his
heart, Gray has murdered himself by killing his soul.
The character of Gladys Hallward, played by Donna
Reed, was an addition to the film version. The niece
of the artist, she falls in love with Gray, despite
the warnings of friends.

Review excerpts: Bosley Crowther of the New York
Times (3/2/45, p. 15) blasted the film for its
"mawkish pomposity" and "utterly artless distortion
of the novel's more meaningful scenes." "Donna Reed
is presented in the flat role of Basil Hallward's
invented niece."

From Variety (3/7/45, p. 20), the film received a
more favorable report, being called "an interesting
and daring experiment." "Another sympathetic
character is Donna Reed, who also falls in love with
Gray but is brushed aside."

The Life (3/19/45, p. 99-102) review called this a
"morbid, unusual film" and made no mention of Donna.

Additional reviews: Commonweal, 3/16/45, p. 543-4;
Cosmopolitan, 5/45, p. 92; Film Daily, 2/26/45, p. 6;
Hollywood Reporter, 2/26/45, p.3; London Times,
5/2/45, p. 6; Magill's Survey of the Cinema I, vol.
3, p. 1335-38, by Alain Silver; New Yorker, 3/10/45,
p. 48; Saturday Review, 3/10/45, p. 24-5; Scholastic,
3/19/45, p. 23; Time, 3/12/45, p. 94

F17.   **THEY WERE EXPENDABLE**   (135 min., B/W)

Metro-Goldwyn-Mayer, 1945
Producer: John Ford
Director: John Ford/Robert Montgomery
Screenplay: Frank Wead
Based on a novel by: William L. White

Cast: Robert Montgomery (*Lt. John Brickley*), John
Wayne (*Lt. Rusty Ryan*), Donna Reed (*2nd Lt. Sandy
Davyss*), Jack Holt (*General Martin*), Ward Bond (*Boats
Mulcahey*), Paul Langton (*Ensign Andy Andrews*), Leon
Ames (*Major James Morton*), Charles Trowbridge
(*Admiral Blackwell*)

Synopsis: Based on the experiences of Lt. John
Bulkeley, a friend of John Ford.   Plot concerns the
Philippine Campaign for Bataan and Corregidor in
1942.   Lieutenants John Brickley and Rusty Ryan are
in command of a squadron of PT boats stationed in
Manila Bay.   Brickley believes in the power and
importance of the PT destroyers, while Ryan feels
they are insignificant, and longs for more important
duties.   Their significance is tested when the
Japanese invade the Bay.   Ryan is injured in the
first attack and is sent to sick bay, where he meets
nurse Sandy Davyss.   Sparks fly between the gruff
Ryan and the equally strong willed nurse. Though he
treats her brusquely, she falls in love with him, and
they eventually find their way together.   Their
romance is short-lived however, as they are
reassigned to separate posts.   The glorious success
of the PT crews fighting off the Japanese invasion
forces causes Brickley and Ryan to be flown to
Australia to organize and train more PT squadrons.

Review excerpts: New York Times (12/21/45, p. 25, by
Bosley Crowther): "Donna Reed is extraordinarily
touching in the role of an Army nurse who figures
into the story in a brief romance which is most
tastefully and credibly handled, by the way."

Variety (11/21/45, p. 10): "Love interest is built
around Wayne and an Army nurse, played appealingly by
Donna Reed."

New York Herald Tribune (12/21/45, by Howard Barnes):
"Donna has the somewhat ambiguous role of an Army
nurse, but she keeps an expedient romance far less
objectionable than it might have been."

Additional reviews: Commonweal, 12/28/45, p. 288;
Film Daily, 11/23/43, p. 6; Hollywood Reporter,
11/19/45, p.3; Life, 12/31/45, p. 61-62; Magill's
Survey of Cinema I, vol. 4, p. 1698-1702; New Yorker,
12/22/45, p. 50; Newsweek, 12/31/45, p. 94; Time,
12/24/45, p. 98

See also: B11 ("Donna Up to Date") includes quotes
by John Ford regarding Donna's work in this film.

F18.   *FAITHFUL IN MY FASHION*   (81 min., B/W)

Metro-Goldwyn-Mayer, 1946
Producer: Lionel Houser
Director: Sidney Salkow
Screenplay: Lionel Houser

Cast: Donna Reed (*Jean Kendrick*), Tom Drake (*Jeff
Compton*), Edward Everett Horton (*Hiram Dilworthy*),
Spring Byington (*Miss Swanson*), Sig Ruman (*Prof.
Boris Riminoffsky*), Harry Davenport (*Great Grandpa*),
William Phillips (*1st Barfly*), Margaret Hamilton
(*Miss Applegate*), Connie Gilchrist (*Mrs. Murphy*)

Synopsis: A soldier comes home on a two week furlough, and his girlfriend puts on a charade in order to make his homecoming a happy one. She has become engaged to another man, but on the advice of coworkers, doesn't tell him. She soon falls back in love with the soldier, but when he learns of her deception he ends the romance. The interfering coworkers again conspire to get the two back together.

Review excerpts: From **Variety** (6/12/46): "Donna Reed makes an appealing heart interest" in this "hokey story."

See also: In the May 1946 issue of **Silver Screen Magazine** (see B1), Donna said of this film, "Why it's the first time I've been able to laugh on the screen!"

F19.   *IT'S A WONDERFUL LIFE*   (129 min., B/W)

RKO/Liberty Films, 1946
Producer: Frank Capra
Director: Frank Capra
Screenplay: Frances Goodrich, Albert Hackett & Frank Capra; additional scenes by Jo Swerling

Cast: James Stewart (*George Bailey*), Donna Reed (*Mary Hatch Bailey*), Lionel Barrymore (*Potter*), Thomas Mitchell (*Uncle Billy*), Beaulah Bondi (*Mrs. Bailey*), Frank Faylen (*Ernie*), Ward Bond (*Bert*), Henry Travers (*Clarence Oddbody*), H.B. Warner (*Mr. Gower*), Gloria Grahame (*Violet*), Samuel S. Hinds (*Pa Bailey*), Sheldon Leonard (*Nick*), Mary Treen (*Cousin Tilly*), Carol Coomes (*Janie Bailey*), Karolyn Grimes (*Zuzu Bailey*), Jimmy Hawkins (*Tommy Bailey*), Carl "Alfafa" Switzer (*Freddie*)

Synopsis: George Bailey, a small town man with big dreams, is driven to despair when disappointment with his life is compounded with the threat of financial ruin. On Christmas Eve, as George is contemplating suicide, the powers that be in Heaven are discussing his situation. They choose an angel to go to Earth to save George's soul. Critical points in George's life up to that point are shown in flashbacks: how he saved his younger brother's life, how he prevented the druggist from accidentally poisoning a child, how young Mary Hatch vowed that she would love him until the day she died. After high school, George works in his father's Building and Loan Association, saving his money for college and travel. The night before he is to leave for Europe, he is returning from a dance with Mary Hatch when he learns that his father has had a stroke. After his father's death the Building and Loan is in danger of being liquidated, but the Board of Directors votes to stay in business if George takes over. If the Building and Loan goes out of business, the entire town would be controlled by

Mr. Potter, the greedy old banker. George stays, sacrificing his college savings so that his brother Harry could go instead. When Harry graduates, George plans to travel the world and leave tiny Bedford Falls behind. Harry returns with a wife, and a better business opportunity, which George presses him to accept. Once again, George stays in Bedford Falls to run the Building & Loan. One night, when George learns that Mary Hatch is home from college, he stops by her place. George is reluctant to admit his feelings for her, seeing her and marriage in general as another trap to keep him in Bedford Falls. When they are both listening to a conversation over the same phone receiver, he can no longer deny his emotions. Soon they are married, and about to leave on their honeymoon. As they are driving out of town they pass the bank and discover that the townspeople are rioting. In order to save the Savings and Loan from being closed and taken over by Potter, they must satisfy all of their customers and keep the doors open until the close of business. George and Mary sacrifice their honeymoon money to save the Building & Loan. At the end of the day, with two dollars left, the doors close and the Bailey Building & Loan is still in business. Once again George Bailey has lost his chance to see the world. He and Mary settle into an old run down house which they fix up. In time they start a family. As the years pass George becomes more and more disillusioned with his life, never having fulfilled his ambitions of travel and adventure. The war comes and George's brother Harry becomes a celebrated hero. George is classified 4F because of a bad ear, and stays at home running the Building & Loan. On the day of Harry's return to Bedford Falls, George's uncle and partner, Billy is making the bank deposit when he sees Potter and gloats to him over Harry's heroism. He then accidentally hands the money, eight thousand dollars, over to Potter in a rolled up newspaper. When Uncle Billy can't find the money, not only is the Building & Loan in trouble, but with the bank inspector in town, George faces the possibility of arrest. It is on this night that George stands on a bridge, contemplating suicide. Clarence Oddbody, the angel (minus wings) who receives the assignment to save George's soul, decides to show George what it would be like if he had never been born. A walk through town reveals that Bedford Falls is now Pottersville and run entirely by Potter. In the cemetery he finds his brother Harry's grave. He learns that since he wasn't there to save Harry when he fell through the ice, Harry died, and since Harry wasn't there to save the lives of a squadron of men in the war, the men died. The druggist whom he wasn't able to prevent from poisoning a child instead went to prison. Mary Hatch became an old maid librarian, and screams when George grabs her. No one, including Mary, recognizes George. Finally realizing how important his life is, and how many other lives he touched, George begs Clarence to bring him back to life. He gets his wish, and returns

home running through the streets shouting "Merry
Christmas" to everyone. When he reaches his house, he
embraces his family and sees the bank examiner.
"Isn't it wonderful? I'm going to jail!" he exclaims.
Friends neighbors and relatives begin showing up at
the house. They heard George was in trouble and they
all showed up to help. They begin emptying their
pockets into a basket, raising more than enough to
bail George out. When a bell on the Christmas tree
rings, daughter Zuzu tells George, "teacher says
every time a bell rings, an angel gets his wings."
George winks up at heaven and says "Attaboy,
Clarence."

Review excerpts, now and then:
The Art of the American Film 1900-1971 (1973, p. 195,
   by Charles Higham): "the most brilliantly made
   motion picture of the 1940s so assured, so
   dazzling is its use of screen narrative."
Commonweal (1/3/47, p. 305, by Philip T. Hartung):
   "an outstanding example of Americana."
Halliwell's Film Guide (New York: Charles Scribner's
   Sons, 1983): "superbly assembled small-town comedy
   drama in a fantasy framework; arguably Capra's
   best work."
Life (12/30/46, p. 68-73): "a masterful edifice of
   comedy and sentiment." "James Stewart...seems
   about the best leading man in pictures. Donna Reed
   is hardly less satisfactory as his wife." (This
   review includes a thirteen photo recap of the
   film.)
Motion Picture Guide (Chicago: Cinebooks, Inc.,
   1986): "Reed is excellent as the loyal, trusting
   wife who knew since childhood she would be Mrs.
   George Bailey."
Nation (2/15/47, p. 193, by James Agee): "one of the
   most efficient sentimental pieces since 'A
   Christmas Carol.'"
New York Times (12/23/46, p. 19, by Bosley Crowther)
   "Donna Reed is remarkably poised and gracious as
   his adoring sweetheart and wife." "the weakness
   of this picture...is the sentimentality of it- its
   illusory concept of life."
New Yorker (12/21/46, p. 87): "so mincing as to
   border on baby talk."
Newsweek (12/30/46): "sentimental, but so expertly
   written, directed and acted that you want to
   believe it."
TV Guide (12/16/89, p. 19): "the most successful
   holiday film of them all, a seasonal treat that
   seems to gain more fans with each passing year."
Time (12/23/46, p. 54): "'It's a Wonderful Life' is a
   pretty wonderful movie. It has only one formidable
   rival (Goldwyn's 'Best Years of Our Lives') as
   Hollywood's best picture of the year."
Variety (12/25/46, p. 12): "'It's a Wonderful Life'
   will enjoy just that at the box office, and
   eminently deserves to do so." "In femme lead,
   Donna Reed will reach full-fledged stardom with
   this effort."

Additional reviews:
Cosmopolitan, 1/47, p. 66+; Film Daily, 12/19/46, p.
5; Films In Review, 4/51, p. 32-38; Hollywood
Reporter, 12/19/46, p. 3; Magill's Survey of Cinema
I, vol. 2, p. 856-9, by DeWitt Bodeen; Photoplay,
3/47, p. 4; Theatre Arts, 2/47, p. 36-37

Other references:
American Film, October 1978, p. 39-51.
Basinger, Jeanine. The "It's A Wonderful Life" Book.
     New York: Alfred A. Knopf, 1986., p. 9-12, 44.
Capra, Frank. The Name Above the Title, New York:
     Macmillan & Co., 1971, p. 376-384.
Ebert, Roger.   "'It's A Wonderful Life': Don't Miss
     Jimmy Stewart Talking to the Shrubbery- or Donna
     Reed Losing Her Bathrobe." TV Guide, 12/24/88, p.
     4-6.
Goodrich, Francis, Albert Hackett and Frank Capra.
     It's A Wonderful Life: St. Martin's original
     screenplay series. New York: St. Martin's Press,
     1986. The complete script in its original form.
Osborne, Robert.   "Rambling Reporter" column,
     Hollywood Reporter, 1/15/86. (see B210)
     Donna's frustration and hurt at being blamed for
     the box office failure of It's a Wonderful Life is
     related by Osborne in this obituary.
Willis, Donald C.   The Films of Frank Capra,
     Metuchen, N.J.: Scarecrow Press, Inc., p. 59-86.
Wolfe, Charles.   Frank Capra Guide to References and
     Resources, Boston: G.K. Hall Co., 1987.

Academy Award nominations: Best Picture, Best
Director, Best Actor (Stewart).

F20.   *GREEN DOLPHIN STREET*   (140 min., B/W)

Metro-Goldwyn-Mayer, 1947
Producer: Carey Wilson
Director: Victor Saville
Screenplay: Samson Raphaelson
Based on the novel by: Elizabeth Goudge

Cast: Lana Turner (*Marianne Patourel*), Van Heflin
(*Timothy Haslam*), Donna Reed (*Marguerite Patourel*),
Richard Hart (*William Ozanne*), Frank Morgan (*Dr.
Edmond Ozanne*), Edmund Gwenn (*Octavius Patourel*),
Dame May Whitty (*Mother Superior*), Reginald Owen
(*Captain O'Hara*), Gladys Cooper (*Sophie Patourel*),
Gigi Perreau (*Veronica*)

Synopsis: Marianne and Marguerite Patourel are two
sisters who fall in love with the same man. William
Ozanne, the object of their mutual attraction, is the
son of the man their mother once loved but didn't
marry. Marianne, the headstrong, aggressive sister,
employs every tactic she can to win William's
affections, while Marguerite, the sweet and gentle
sister patiently waits and hopes he'll choose her.
He does, but they keep their feelings secret while he

goes off and joins the Navy in order to become an
officer and a gentleman. Years later he settles in
New Zealand, and in a drunken state, writes home to
ask the girls' father permission to marry his
sweetheart. In a "slip of the pen" he writes
Marianne's name in the letter rather than
Marguerite's. When Marianne shows up, after a long
and perilous journey by sea, William can't admit his
mistake, and he marries her. Back home, Marguerite
is devastated by her loss and turns to the church for
guidance. Through the years William and Marianne
become successful in business, but their marriage
built on lies goes through troubled times. They
return to their home many years later with their
daughter, just before Marguerite is to take her final
vows as a nun. Marianne finds a letter William had
written to Marguerite years before and learns that it
was her sister that her husband really loved. She
confronts William that night and he confesses his
mistake and the reason he married her, but contends
that over the years he has grown to love her
(Marianne) and wants to save his marriage. She goes
to Marguerite and tells her sister that William wrote
the wrong name in the proposal letter, and that she
should go to William, rather than become a nun. But
Marguerite has found what she was missing in life,
and William had nothing to do with it. William
finally convinces Marianne that he loves her and not
her sister, and they reconcile.

Review excerpts: Reviewers largely agreed that the
screenplay was weak, and the plot hinging on a "slip
of the pen" hard to swallow. Donna's performance was
given lukewarm notices. Bosley Crowther of the New
York Times (10/16/47, p. 34) called Donna "durable."

Variety (10/22/47, p. 12): "As the gentler of the
sisters, Miss Reed is bogged by the weight of the
yarn. Patly performing in the early reels, she fails
to turn the hazardous trick of making her later
conversion credible."

Time (11/3/47, p. 100) observed: "Donna Reed is the
sweet sister. You can tell because she flutters her
eyelashes...Moral seems to be: if you want to be
happy, be sure to marry someone you don't love."

Additional reviews: Commonweal, 10/31/47, p. 71;
Film Daily, 10/16/47, p. 8; Hollywood Reporter,
10/16/47, p. 8; New Republic, 10/27/47, p. 36; New
Yorker, 10/25/47, p. 94; Newsweek, 10/27/47, p. 96

See also: The Hollywood Reporter on 1/15/86 (B216)
contains an interesting sidenote. June Allyson was
first offered the role of Marguerite, but turned it
down. Donna also didn't want the role in the
beginning, claiming that no one would believe Hart's
character chose her over Lana Turner. "Lana's
gorgeous. If I play that part, it'll ruin the
picture."

Donna called Marguerite Patourel "The Role I Liked Best" in a 1951 article (see B84).

F21.   *BEYOND GLORY*   (82 min., B/W)

Paramount, 1948
Producer: Robert Fellows
Director: John Farrow
Screenplay: Jonathan Latimer, Charles Marquis Warren, William Wister Haines

Cast: Alan Ladd (*Rockwell "Rocky" Gilman*), Donna Reed (*Ann Daniels*), George Macready (*Major General Bond*), George Coulouris (*Lew Proctor*), Harold Vermilyea (*Raymond Denmore, Sr.*), Henry Travers (*Pop Dewing*), Luis Van Rooten (*Dr. White*), Tom Neal (*Henry Daniels*), Conrad Janis (*Raymond Denmore, Jr.*), Audie Murphy (*Thomas*), Dick Hogan (*Cadet Sgt. Eddie Loughlin*)

Synopsis: Cadet "Rocky" Gilman believes himself responsible for the death of his commanding officer, Henry Daniels, because he blacked out during a key battle in Tunisia seconds before Daniels was killed. His guilt haunts him and after his discharge he visits the man's widow, Ann. The two fall in love, and with her encouragement, Gilman enters West Point. Meanwhile, Raymond Denmore, Jr., a former cadet whose discharge was based on Gilman's testimony is brought to trial for his crimes. The defense attorney tries to discredit Gilman's testimony by portraying him as a coward, unworthy of his West Point uniform. To his detriment, Gilman seems reluctant to defend himself, due to his guilty conscience. Cadet Loughlin, who was present during the Tunisian attack, reveals on the witness stand that Gilman did not panic, but was rather knocked unconscious by enemy artillery just before Daniels' death, and Gilman's honor is restored.

Review excerpts: While the film itself garnered only mild reviews, Donna's presence was repeatedly counted among its virtues:

New York Times (8/4/48, p. 18 by Thomas F. Brady): "Donna Reed... is creditably restrained in her depiction of a war widow."

Variety (6/16/48): "Donna Reed lends a quiet charm as the war widow who believes in Ladd."

Time (8/9/48, p. 74): "It is filmed with romantic feeling for place and protocol, and there are appropriate performances by Ladd... and by Miss Reed, the screen's All American Nice Girl."

Additional Reviews: Commonweal, 8/20/48, p. 454; Newsweek, 8/16/48, p. 76

F22.   *CHICAGO DEADLINE*   *(87 min., B/W)*

Paramount, 1949
Producer: Robert Fellows
Director: Lewis Allen
Screenplay: Warren Duff
Based on the novel "One Woman" by: Tiffany Thayer

Cast: Alan Ladd (*Ed Adams*), Donna Reed (*Rosita Jean D'ur*), June Havoc (*Leona*), Irene Hervey (*Belle Dorset*), Arthur Kennedy (*Tommy Ditman*), Berry Kroeger (*Solly Wellman*), Harold Vermilyea (*Anstruder*), Shepperd Strudwick (*Blacky Franchot*), John Beal (*Paul Jean D'Ur*), Dave Willock (*Pig*)

Synopsis: A young woman is found dead of tuberculosis in a cheap rooming house by a reporter, who happened to be in the next room. Before the police arrive, the reporter takes the girl's address book and sets out on his own to learn more about her life. He tracks down various people in her life, from gangsters to hookers to a ruthless banker, who tell stories in flashbacks of her. He pieces together the heart-breaking story of her life, uncovering several murders and blackmail victims along the way. He confronts the culprit of those crimes, Solly Wellman, in a final shootout in which Wellman is killed and Adams, the reporter, is wounded. Adams later leaves his hospital bed to attend the girl's funeral. Over the course of his investigation he has become enraptured with the dead girl and he burns her address book in order to protect her memory.

Review excerpts: The dismal review given to this film by Bosley Crowther of the New York Times (11/3/49, p. 37) proclaimed it a "mish-mosh of two-penny-fiction cliches, recklessly thrown together in an almost unfathomable plot." Donna's performance is not critiqued.

In a more favorable review, Variety (8/31/49) said of Donna Reed, "she gives an appealing performance."

Additional reviews: Commonweal, 12/16/49, p. 294; Good Housekeeping, 12/49, p. 238; Newsweek, 11/21/49, p. 93; Photoplay, 11/49, p. 20

F23.   *SATURDAY'S HERO*   *(109 min., B/W)*

Columbia Pictures, 1951
Producer: Buddy Adler
Director: David Miller
Screenplay: Millard Lampbell and Sidney Buchman
Based on novel "The Hero" by: Millard Lampbell

Cast: John Derek (*Steve Novak*), Donna Reed (*Melissa*), Sidney Blackmer (*T.C. McCabe*), Alexander Knox (*Megroth*), Elliott Lewis (*Eddie Abrams*), Otto Hulett (*Coach Tennant*), Howard St. John (*Belfrage*)

Synopsis: A poor high school boy is given a football scholarship to a Southern college. He begins with good intentions to raise himself above his humble beginnings by studying hard and playing his best. However, his coach and other advisors view college ball as a business rather than sport, and he isn't given time to learn anything. When he is injured in his third year and can no longer play ball, he soon learns that his value to the school was purely commercial. He regains his self-respect by getting a job and settling down with his girlfriend, while also attending night school.

Review excerpts: "Donna Reed plays the girl with standard radiance."   (Bosley Crowther, New York Times, 9/21/51, p. 37.)

Additional reviews: Commonweal, 10/12/51, p. 14; Film Daily, 8/23/51, p. 6; Hollywood Reporter, 8/22/51, p. 3; Nation, 9/29/51, p. 267-8; Newsweek, 9/10/51, p. 98+; Time, 10/15/51, p. 122

F24.   *SCANDAL SHEET*   (82 min., B/W)

Columbia Pictures, 1952
Producer: Edward Small
Director: Phil Karlson
Screenplay: Ted Sherdeman, Eugene Ling, James Poe
Based on the novel "The Dark Page" by: Samuel Fuller

Cast: Broderick Crawford (*Mark Chapman*), John Derek (*Steve McCleary*), Donna Reed (*Julie Allison*), Rosemary DeCamp (*Charlotte Grant*), Henry O'Neill (*Charlie Barnes*), Henry Morgan (*Biddle*), James Millican (*Lt. Davis*), Griff Barnett (*Judge Hacker*)

Synopsis: Newspaper editor Mark Chapman is made responsible for generating more sales for the "New York Express" in order to save the paper from bankruptcy. Chapman decides to turn the once well-respected paper into a tabloid. Relying on sensational headlines and questionable reporting techniques, he manages to propel the paper's circulation through the roof. Steve McCleary, Chapman's protege, admires his bosses achievement, but his girlfriend Julie Allison, a feature writer, ardently objects. When Chapman's fame and fortune are jeopardized by the sudden appearance of the wife he deserted years ago, he panics. The woman is now penniless and threatens to expose Chapman as a deserter. Chapman becomes enraged and beats her to death, then removes all traces of her identity from her apartment.   When the murder is discovered, McCleary decides to investigate in order to impress his boss. His friend, reporter Charlie Barnes, turns up a photograph of Chapman and the woman, but is murdered by Chapman before he can tell McCleary. When McCleary and Allison finally discover the woman's identity, Chapman turns up with a gun, threatening to

shoot. The police arrive and Chapman is killed in the
ensuing shootout. McCleary, no longer a fan of
tabloid journalism or Chapman's tactics, writes his
boss' obituary for the front page.

Review excerpts: Variety's (1/9/52, p. 6) appraisal
of the film was mildly favorable, and Donna Reed's
performance is judged "credible."

Bosley Crowther of The New York Times (1/17/52, p.
23) lambasted the film and cast. He commented that
"Donna Reed watches on with dull disfavor as a Vassar
girl who has stumbled into a tabloid job."

Additional reviews: Film Daily, 1/15/52, p. 6;
Hollywood Reporter, 1/9/52, p. 3; Newsweek, 1/28/52,
p. 89; Time, 2/4/52, p. 72

F25.   *HANGMAN'S KNOT*   (80 min., Color)

Columbia Pictures, 1952
Producer: Harry Joe Brown
Director: Roy Huggins
Screenplay: Roy Huggins

Cast: Randolph Scott (Matt Stewart), Donna Reed
(Molly Hull), Claude Jarman, Jr. (Jamie Groves),
Frank Faylen (Cass Browne), Glenn Langan (Capt.
Peterson), Richard Denning (Lee Kemper), Lee Marvin
(Rolph Bainter), Jeanette Nolan (Mrs. Harris)

Synopsis: Matt Stewart leads a Confederate raiding
party at the end of the Civil War. After robbing a
Union gold shipment in the Nevada Territory, they
learn that the war has been over for a month. They
further discover that they stand to face criminal
charges for felony and murder, acts committed while
they thought a war was on. Their decision to take the
gold with them to help rebuild the South proves a
dangerous one, as lawmen and civilians alike are
after the gold and no one believes they didn't know
the war had ended. The group is trapped in a stage
station by a group of greedy renegades posing as
deputies. Molly Hull is one of four hostages the
groups holds at the station. A Union nurse, she takes
care of one of the men who is injured. Defiant at
first, she later believes in the innocence of the
Confederate group and grows fond of Stewart. The
group's first attempt to escape is thwarted by Lee
Kemper, Molly's traveling companion, who breaks his
promise to keep quiet. The bandits try to get the
Confederates out by setting fire to the station. A
flash thunderstorm gives Stewart and his men a chance
to escape but in the ensuing battle most are killed.
In the aftermath, Stewart leaves for the South,
promising to return for Molly. So as not to be
branded an outlaw, he leaves the gold behind to be
returned to its rightful owners.

Review excerpts: Reviewers praised both the film and Donna' performance. From the New York Times (12/11/52, p. 45): "It is a tight little entertainment which does justice to this film form." From the same review, "Donna Reed...is utterly natural as her hate is turned to admiration when she comes to know her captor better."

Variety (10/29/52) called the film a "slambang western" in its very favorable review. Direction, script, technical work and the entire cast are commended. "Miss Reed is excellent as the ex-Union Army nurse who tends Scott's wounded men."

Additional reviews: Newsweek, 12/22/52, p. 72; National Parent-Teacher, 1/53, p. 38

F26.   **TROUBLE ALONG THE WAY**   (110 min., B/W)

Warner Brothers, 1953
Producer: Melville Shavelson
Director: Michael Curtiz
Screenplay: Melville Shavelson and Jack Rose
Story by: Douglas Morrow and Robert Hardy Andrews

Cast: John Wayne (*Steve Aloysius Williams*), Donna Reed (*Alice Singleton*), Charles Coburn (*Father Burke*), Tom Tully (*Father Malone*), Sherry Jackson (*Carole Williams*), Marie Windsor (*Anne McCormick*), Tom Helmore (*Harold McCormick*), Dabbs Greer (*Father McCormick*)

Synopsis: St. Anthony's college is in danger of being closed unless Father Burke can raise the $170,000 needed to pay off the school's debts. He decides that a winning football team can bring in the revenue, and sets out to find a good coach. He recruits Steve Williams, a cynical ex-coach known for his nonconformity. Williams takes the job to favorably impress a probations officer sent to judge whether he is a good father to his young daughter. Williams puts together a championship team, but his methods are not quite above-board. From dishonest recruiting practices to ill-gotten equipment, Williams will do anything to insure a winning team and keep his daughter. When the honest Father Burke learns of Williams' disreputable methods, he cancels the remainder of the games. Alice Singleton, the probations officer who has taken a personal interest in both Williams and his young daughter, withdraws her favorable report when she hears the truth. A custody trial takes place, and it looks as though Williams will lose his daughter to his ex-wife and her new husband. Father Burke shows up and testifies that it was his fault Williams behaved as he did, he had made such tough demands on the coach. He offers Williams his job back and the coach is able to regain custody of his daughter, and win back the affections of Singleton.

Review excerpts: A.H. Weiler's review for the New York Times (5/7/53, p. 37) called the film "a scoring entertainment" in which "Donna Reed is pretty and intellectual as the probation officer who is assigned to investigate, but loses her heart to Wayne."

Variety (3/18/53) offered: "Donna Reed gives her role as a probation officer all that it needs to hold its own with the two male stars, besides being a looker."

Additional reviews: Commonweal, 4/24/53, p. 73; New York Herald Tribune, 5/7/53; Newsweek, 4/13/53, p. 108; Saturday Review 4/18/53, p. 30; Time, 4/20/53

F27. *RAIDERS OF THE SEVEN SEAS* (87 min., Color)

United Artists, 1953
Producer: Sidney Salkow
Director: Sidney Salkow
Screenplay: John O'Dea, Sidney Salkow
Based on a story by: John O'Dea, Sidney Salkow

Cast: John Payne (*Barbarossa*), Donna Reed (*Alida*), Gerald Mohr (*Salcedo*), Lon Chaney, Jr. (*Peg Leg*), Anthony Caruso (*Renzo*), Henry Brandon (*Capt. Goiti*), Skip Torgerson (*Datu*)

Synopsis: Red-bearded pirate Barbarossa takes over a Spanish prison ship, liberates the prisoners, and recruits them as his crew. He takes on the Spanish fleet, and romances Alida, the fiancee' of Spanish officer Salcedo. The spirited Alida manages to escape, but later realizes she loves Barbarossa, and sabotages Salcedo's plot to capture the pirate ship. As Barbarossa sails for North America with Alida and his crew, Salcedo is left humiliated.

Review excerpts: Variety (4/29/53) called the film a "good pirate adventure" with an "entertaining" plot. The reviewer continues, "Donna Reed cuts a beautiful figure in costumes of the period."

F28. *FROM HERE TO ETERNITY* (118 min., B/W)

Columbia Pictures, 1953
Producer: Buddy Adler
Director: Fred Zinnemann
Screenplay: Daniel Taradash
Based on the novel by: James Jones

Cast: Burt Lancaster (*Sgt. Milton Warden*), Montgomery Clift (*Robert E. Lee Prewitt*), Deborah Kerr (*Karen Holmes*), Frank Sinatra (*Angelo Maggio*), Donna Reed (*Alma 'Lorene'*), Ernest Borgnine (*Sergeant Judson*), Philip Ober (*Captain Dana Holmes*), Mickey Shaughnessy (*Sergeant Leva*), Harry Bellaver (*Mazzioli*), Jack Warden (*Corporal Buckley*), John Dennis (*Sergeant Ike Galovitch*)

Synopsis: Set in the army base at Pearl Harbor, the film follows the events in several soldiers' lives leading up to the Japanese attack on December 7, 1941. Private Robert E. Lee Prewitt arrives at the base, having been transferred from his previous post because he refused to continue being the company boxer.   His new commander, Captain Dana Holmes, a ruthless, career minded officer, approaches Prewitt to fight for the company's team.   Prewitt declines, even when Holmes offers him the post of bugler, a job Prewitt very much desires.   It is revealed that Prewitt vowed never to fight again after a bout in which he blinded his best friend.   Holmes, greedy for a promotion and a prize winning team, orders his top sergeant, Milton Warden, to bear down on Prewitt harshly until the soldier relents.   Prewitt is given every dirty work detail in the company, but obstinately refuses to give in.   Befriending Prewitt is Angelo Maggio, a street-tough Italian private with a penchant for trouble-making.   The two friends frequent the New Congress Club, a dance hall where Prewitt meets Lorene, a hostess.   (A prostitute in the James Jones novel, the character was softened for the film.   Her activities as a "hostess" are left unclear.)   Another relationship is heating up between Warden and his captain's wife, Karen Holmes.   Her husband is cheating also, and their marriage is a very shaky one.   Warden and his mistress meet secretly in a variety of settings including the now famous beach scene.   Both make promises of a future together, but his devotion to the Army stands in their way.   Captain Holmes is later relieved of his command for standing by and doing nothing while Prewitt and another soldier fight in the streets. Meanwhile, Maggio's wise-cracking gets him into a barroom brawl with "Fatso" Judson, and he makes a deadly enemy of the bulky sergeant of the stockade. When Maggio is sent to the stockade for another offense, he is subject to merciless beatings by Judson.   He manages to escape and finds Prewitt.   He tells his friend of his brutal treatment, and then dies in his arms.   Prewitt vows revenge upon Judson, and gets his chance soon after.   He lures Judson into an alley and the two fight, both armed with switchblades.   As a result of their struggle, Prewitt is wounded, and Judson is killed.   Prewitt flees, taking refuge at Lorene's apartment while he recuperates.   Warden, who has taken over command of the post, marks Prewitt present rather than report him as being AWOL, believing him to be "the best damned soldier I ever knew" and not wanting to ruin Prewitt's career.   When the bombings on Pearl Harbor begin, Prewitt leaves Lorene's to rejoin his unit, despite her desperate pleadings for him to stay and make a life with her.   His loyalties are with the Army, and though still wounded, he races back to the base.   Not stopping to identify himself to soldiers on guard against Japanese forces, he is shot and killed.   The final shot is of Karen Holmes and Lorene departing the island by boat, and discussing their

lost loves. Lorene lies about what Prewitt did and
how he died, and vows never to return, as they toss
their leis onto the water and watch them float away.

Review excerpts: "From Here to Eternity" received
outstanding reviews, including the New York Times'
(8/6/53, p. 16) evaluation, which called it a
"shining example of truly professional moviemaking"
with "scope, power and impact." Reviewer A.H. Weiler
added that "While Donna Reed is not precisely the
picture of a lady of the evening, her delineation of
Lorene, wracked between a desire to be "proper" and
her anomalous affair with Prewitt, is polished and
professional."

Variety's (7/29/53, p. 6) indepth review praised
director, screenplay, and cast and called the film
"an outstanding motion picture." Donna Reed "has a
change of pace and reveals an ability for meaty,
dramatic work scarcely suspected from her previous
assignments."

Additional reviews: America, 8/15/53, p. 486;
Collier's, 8/7/53, p. 38-9; Films in Review, 10/53,
p. 428-30; Harper's, 10/53, p. 92-3; Holiday, 1/54,
p. 14; Hollywood Reporter, 7/29/53, p. 3; Life,
8/31/53, p. 81-3; Look, 8/25/53, p. 41-3; McCall's,
10/53, p. 8; Nation, 8/29/53, p. 178; New Yorker,
8/8/53, p. 51; Newsweek, 8/10/53, p. 82; Saturday
Review, 8/8/53, p. 25; Time, 8/10/53, p. 94

Academy Awards: Donna Reed won her Best Supporting
Actress Oscar for her role (see A2). In addition, the
film won Best Motion Picture, Best Screenplay, Best
Director, Best Sound Recording, Best Film Editing and
Frank Sinatra won Best Supporting Actor. Nominees
included: Burt Lancaster, Montgomery Clift, and
Deborah Kerr

See also: King Cohn (B259), the biography of Columbia
Studio boss Harry Cohn, for an account of Donna's
casting in the film.

F29.   *THE CADDY*   (95 min., B/W)

Paramount, 1953
Producer: Paul Jones
Director: Norman Taurog
Screenplay: Edmund Hartmann & Danny Arnold
Additional dialog by: Ken Englund
Based on story by: Danny Arnold

Cast: Dean Martin (*Joe Anthony*), Jerry Lewis (*Harvey
Miller*), Donna Reed (*Kathy Taylor*), Barbara Bates
(*Lisa Anthony*), Joseph Calleia (*Papa Anthony*), Fred
Clark (*Mr. Baxter*), Clinton Sundberg (*Charles*),
Howard Smith (*Golf Official*), Marshall Thompson
(*Bruce Reeber*), Marjorie Gateson (*Mrs. Taylor*), Frank
Puglia (*Mr. Spezzato*), Lewis Martin (*Mr. Taylor*)

Synopsis: Harvey Miller, a good-hearted but clumsy fellow, loses his job and longs to be a pro golfer like his father. Fear of crowds prevents him from competing, but he teams up with Joe Anthony, his girlfriend's brother who is looking to make a quick buck. Anthony has immediate success, and steps on his caddy/manager Miller on the way up. After Miller inadvertently entangles Anthony's romance with a rich society girl, (Kathy Taylor, played by Donna Reed) the two are through as a team. Anthony tries to go it alone, but at the big tournament Miller's clumsiness and Anthony's family driving onto the golf course turn the event into a fiasco, and Anthony is barred from competing. All this is told as a flashback as the famous comedy team "Anthony and Miller" are telling a reporter how they got their start in show business. (It seems a talent agent who witnessed their golf course antics "discovered" the pair and made them stars.) Dean Martin and Jerry Lewis sing "That's Amore," "What Wouldcha Do Without Me" and others, and Lewis' hilarious takeoff on "The Gay Continental" is a special treat.

Review excerpts: Bosley Crowther's New York Times (9/18/53, p. 16) review called this a "scatter-brained fiction" and "cut-to-size Martin-Lewis farce" with Jerry Lewis' antics standing out as the highlight. Donna Reed gets an incidental mention, with no critique on her performance.

Variety's reviewer (8/5/53, p. 6) gave the film a favorable review, citing "humor with heart" and "strong comedy routines" adding up to "excellent comedy results." Donna Reed is said to have performed her role "attractively."

Additional reviews: Film Daily, 8/10/53, p. 6; Hollywood Reporter, 8/4/53, p. 3; McCall's, 10/53, p. 10; Time, 9/28/53, p. 84

F30.   *GUN FURY*   (83 min., Color)

Columbia Pictures, 1953
Producer: Lewis J. Rachmil
Director: Raoul Walsh
Screenplay: Irving Wallace and Roy Huggins
Based on the novel "Ten Against Caesar" by: Kathleen B. Granger, George Granger and Robert A. Granger

Cast: Rock Hudson (*Ben Warren*), Donna Reed (*Jennifer Ballard*), Phil Carey (*Frank Slayton*), Roberta Haynes (*Estella Morales*), Leo Gordon (*Jess Burgess*), Lee Marvin (*Blinky*), Neville Brand (*Brazos*), Ray Thomas (*Doc*), Robert Herron (*Curly Jordan*)

Synopsis: Civil war veteran Ben Warren and his fiancee' Jennifer Ballard are heading West when their stagecoach' is ambushed by psychotic outlaw Frank Slayton and his gang. Slayton kidnaps the woman and leaves Warren behind, believing him dead. Warren pursues the gang with the help of others who have a vengeance against Slayton. In his quest for revenge, Warren eventually becomes as crazed as Slayton, and their final showdown proves an exciting match of wills. Filmed in 3-D.

Reviews: Commonweal, 11/27/53, p. 198; National Parent-Teacher, 12/53, p. 39; Newsweek, 10/26/53, p. 116; Time, 12/7/53, p. 110

F31.   *THREE HOURS TO KILL*   (77 min., Color)

Columbia Pictures, 1954
Producer: Harry Joe Brown
Director: Alfred Werker
Screenplay: Richard Alan Simmons, Roy Huggins & Maxwell Shane
Story by: Alex Gottlieb
Cast: Dana Andrews (*Jim Guthrie*), Donna Reed (*Laurie Mastin*), Dianne Foster (*Chris Plumber*), Stephen Elliott (*Ben East*), Richard Coogan (*Niles Hendricks*), Laurence Hugo (*Marty Lasswell*), Richard Webb (*Carter Mastin*), Carolyn Jones (*Polly*), Whit Bissell (*Deke*)

Synopsis: Jim Guthrie is a cowboy wrongly accused of murder. An angry lynch mob nearly kills him, but they set him free to prove his innocence. He vengefully tracks down the guilty party and stands up to the townspeople who scorn and fear him.

Review excerpts: Howard Thompson of the New York Times (9/4/54, p. 6) mused: "It's hard to imagine how Dana Andrews and Donna Reed, the latter still clutching last year's supporting actress Oscar, got involved in the lukewarm little Columbia western... However, the performances are competent enough."

New York Herald Tribune, (9/4/54): "Donna Reed is appropriately teary as the girl he left behind."

Additional Reviews: Film Daily, 9/13/54, p. 6; Hollywood Reporter, 9/8/54, p. 3; Newsweek, 9/6/54, p. 77; Time, 10/18/54, p. 102

F32.   *THEY RODE WEST*   (84 min., Color)

Columbia, 1954
Producer: Lewis J. Rachmil
Director: Phil Karlson
Screenplay: DeVallon Scott, Frank Nugent
Based on a story by: Leo Katcher

Cast: Robert Francis (*Dr. Allen Seward*), Donna Reed (*Laurie MacKaye*), May Wynn (*Manyi-ten*), Phil Carey (*Captain Peter Blake*), Onslow Stevens (*Colonel Ethan Walters*), Peggy Converse (*Mrs. Walters*), Roy Roberts (*Sergeant Creever*), Jack Kelly (*Lt. Raymond*)

Synopsis: Dr. Allen Seward is appointed medical
officer at a western cavalry fort.   As previous
doctors in the position were drunks or incompetents,
the residents distrust the doctor from the start. He
slowly wins their faith by proving himself a capable
doctor. When he disobeys orders and begins treating
members of   the   local Kiowa tribe suffering an
epidemic, he again generates bad feelings among the
soldiers. The situation worsens when the Kiowas join
some Comanches on a raid of the fort.   The doctor
brings about peace in the end by using his medical
skills to help the Kiowas, and proving the tribe
worthy of the soldiers' friendship.

Review excerpts: Variety (10/20/54) called the film
"a cut above standards of most such offerings."
"Along for additional casting emphasis," Donna Reed
"comes over as a flirtatious visitor at the fort."

Additional Reviews: National Parent-Teacher, 12/54,
p. 39

F33.   *THE LAST TIME I SAW PARIS*   (116 min., Color)

Metro-Goldwyn-Mayer, 1954
Producer: Jack Cummings
Director: Richard Brooks
Screenplay: Julius J. Epstein, Philip G. Epstein &
Richard Brooks
Based on F. Scott Fitzgerald's "Babylon Revisited"

Cast: Elizabeth Taylor   (*Helen Ellswirth*), Van
Johnson   (*Charles   Wills*),   Walter Pidgeon (*James
Ellswirth*), Donna Reed (*Marion Ellswirth*), Eva Gabor
(*Lorraine Quarl*), Kurt Kasznar (*Maurice*), George
Dolenz (Claude Matine), Roger Moore (*Paul*), Sandy
Descher (*Vicki*)

Synopsis: Reporter Charlie Wills meets two girls on
V-E day in Paris. The two are sisters, and they both
fall for him. Helen, the wilder of the two, wins his
heart. They marry and raise a child, while sister
Marion, still suffering from unrequited love, marries
Claude Matine. Charlie and Helen's marriage is
troubled from the start, as his failures in writing
turn him into an alcoholic, and her wild ways and
flirtatious manner anger him. They separate and he
romances a rich divorcee', while she becomes involved
with a young tennis pro. One night he returns home
drunk and passes out, accidentally locking Helen out.
She spends the night outside in a snowstorm and
subsequently dies of pneumonia. Marion threatens to
sue for custody of her niece Vicki, claiming that
Charlie is an unfit father. He gives in and returns
to America, leaving Vicki with Marion and Claude. He
returns to Paris some time later a successful
novelist, intent on regaining custody of his
daughter. Marion not only blames Charlie for Helen's
death, but also for choosing Helen over her years

earlier, and she refuses to relinquish custody. After
an emotional confrontation with husband Claude,
Marion realizes she was wrong, and turns the girl
over to her father.

Reviews: <u>Variety</u> (11/3/54, p. 6) called the film "an
engrossing romantic drama", and said of Donna's
performance: "Miss Reed, though with less footage
than most of her co-stars, makes her character of a
girl blighted by an unrequited love entirely
understandable, even sympathetic."

A less favorable review was given by Bosley Crowther
of the <u>New York Times</u> (11/19/54, p. 20), who called
Donna's performance "vapid."

Additional reviews: <u>Commonweal</u>, 11/26/54, p. 223;
<u>Film Daily</u>, 11/4/54, p. 6; <u>Films and Filming</u>, 2/55,
p. 20; <u>Hollywood Reporter</u>, 11/3/54, p. 3; <u>Library
Journal</u>, 12/15/54, p.2438; <u>New Yorker</u>, 12/4/54, p.
227; <u>Newsweek</u>, 11/22/54, p. 106; <u>Saturday Review</u>,
11/20/54, p. 31; <u>Time</u>, 11/22/54, p. 102

F34.   *THE FAR HORIZONS*   (108 min., Color)

Paramount, 1955
Producer: William H. Pine and William C. Thomas
Director: Rudolph Mate'
Screenplay: Winston Miller, Edmund H. North
Based on the novel <u>Sacajawea of the Shoshones</u> by:
Della Gould Emmons

Cast: Fred MacMurray (*Merriwether Lewis*), Charlton
Heston (*Bill Clark*), Donna Reed (*Sacajawea*), Barbara
Hale (*Julia Hancock*), William Demarest (*Sergeant
Cass*), Alan Reed (*Charbonneau*), Larry Pennell (*Wild
Eagle*)

Synopsis: This historical adventure chronicles Lewis
and Clark's expedition through the Louisiana Purchase
territory. The pair are depicted as rivals from the
start, competing for the same woman's attentions.
Clark wins the girl (Julia Hancock, played by Barbara
Hale) before the two leave on their journey. The
expedition party must conquer Indian attacks, brutal
weather and their own feuding before reaching their
destination. Halfway along, a beautiful Shoshone
Indian girl joins the group and acts as their guide.
The now legendary Sacajawea, whose fearless
leadership was instrumental in Lewis and Clark's
success, becomes the focus of the latter part of the
film. According to this account, she falls in love
with Clark, who in turn forgets all about the woman
he left behind. Upon completion of their journey,
Lewis and Clark visit the White House, with Sacajawea
by their side. The Indian decides that despite her
love for Clark, she cannot adapt to life in
civilization, and she returns to her tribe in the
mountains.

Review excerpts: The <u>New York Times</u> review (5/21/55, p. 11) by Howard Thompson called the film a "slow and unimaginative safari" the highlight of which is the "consistently winning performance by Miss Reed."

<u>Variety</u> (5/25/55) further praised Donna's performance: "This copper rose (Sacajawea) is beautifully played by Donna Reed for the only believable character in the picture."

Additional reviews: <u>America</u>, 6/25/55, p. 339; <u>Newsweek</u>, 6/6/55, p. 98; <u>Time</u>, 6/6/55, p. 110

See also: B67 and B81 concern Donna's campaign to get Sacajawea elected to the Hall of Fame.

F35.   ***RANSOM!***   (109 min., B/W)

Metro-Goldwyn-Mayer, 1956
Producer: Nicholas Nayfack
Director: Alex Segal
Screenplay: Cyril Hume, Richard Maibaum

Cast: Glenn Ford (*David G. Stannard*), Donna Reed (*Edith Stannard*), Leslie Nielsen (*Charlie Telfer*), Juano Hernandez (*Jesse Chapman*), Robert Keith (*Chief Jim Backett*), Richard Gaines (*Langly*), Mabel Albertson (*Mrs. Partridge*), Alexander Scourby (*Dr. Paul Y. Gorman*), Bobby Clark (*Andy Stannard*)

Synopsis: The story of a man who refuses to pay ransom money to his son's kidnappers, it was twice produced for television under the title "Fearful Decision" before this film version was made. The same writers and director collaborated on both the film and television productions, but reviewers largely agreed that the material added to stretch it out to feature length also served to lessen the dramatic impact, and the film version was less powerful. In the opening sequence, D.G. Stannard, president of Stannard Industries, finds his young son Andy building a fort using planks stolen from bed-boards. He promises the boy he will leave work early to help him. When Andy doesn't return on the school bus that afternoon, it is discovered that he was kidnapped. The kidnappers demand $500,000 ransom, which is easily raised by Stannard, his brother, and their staff. Stannard then changes his mind and goes on TV demanding the safe return of his son and vowing that the kidnappers will never get one cent from him. Instead, he threatens, the money will be offered as a reward for their capture in the event the boy is harmed. Stannard's wife Edith vehemently opposes her husband's plan, and begs him to turn over the ransom money. When he refuses, she leaves him. His gambit works, and the boy is returned that night, unharmed.

Reviews: Bosley Crowther of the <u>New York Times</u> (1/25/56, p. 28) found the plot to be implausible,

and the performances "fabricated" and "theatrical."
He called Donna Reed "incredibly saccharine and
emotionally unsettled as the wife."

<u>Variety</u>'s reviewer (1/11/56) compared the film to the
television versions and had little to say in favor of
the former. Of the performances, "the direction
fails to get much out of Miss Reed that can be felt
and most of the other players, too, seem at odds with
the characters they play..."

<u>World Telegram</u> (1/25/56, by Alton Cook): "There are
some excellent parts among them, notably Donna Reed
as the frantically distraught mother."

Additional reviews: <u>America</u>, 2/4/56, p. 516;
<u>Commonweal</u>, 2/17/56, p. 516; <u>New Yorker</u>, 2/4/56, p.
66; <u>Newsweek</u>, 1/16/56, p. 80; <u>Saturday Review</u>,
1/28/56, p. 19; <u>Time</u>, 2/13/56, p. 90+.

F36.   *THE BENNY GOODMAN STORY*   (116 min., Color)

Universal, 1956
Producer: Aaron Rosenberg
Director: Valentine Davies
Screenplay: Valentine Davies

Cast: Steve Allen (*Benny Goodman*), Donna Reed (*Alice
Hammond*), Berta Gersten (*Mom Goodman*), Herbert
Anderson (*John Hammond*), Robert F. Simon (*Pop
Goodman*), Sammy Davis, Sr. (*Fletcher Henderson*), Dick
Winslow (*Gil Rodin*), Barry Truex (*Benny Goodman at
16*), Hy Averback (*William Alexander*), Harry James,
Martha Tilton, Gene Krupa

Synopsis: A musical biography of Benny Goodman, the
film follows the band leader's life from early
poverty to fame and fortune. His courtship and
marriage to society girl Alice Hammond (played by
Donna Reed) are played up to give the film some zing
in the romance department. The story apparently
follows history pretty accurately, with some
theatrical improvising by the screenwriter. Many of
the musicians Goodman played with are played by
themselves, and Goodman himself does all of the
actual clarinet playing for Steve Allen.

Review excerpts: Bosley Crowther of the <u>New York
Times</u> (2/22/56, p. 22) warned that the only reason to
see this film is for Benny Goodman's fabulous swing
music played throughout the film. He found nothing
to praise among the performances, and lumped Reed,
Gersten, and Averback, together as being "sluggish."

The <u>Variety</u> reviewer (12/21/55) discussed this film's
prospects in comparison to <u>The Glenn Miller Story</u> by
the same producer, and surmised that it "should
achieve similar box office potency." The two stars
are rated as "believable."

Donna's most flattering praise came from <u>Newsweek</u> (2/6/56, p. 86), whose reviewer stated "as the upper-crust girl whom Goodman married, Donna Reed has little to do and does it glowingly."

Additional Reviews: <u>America</u>, 3/10/56, p. 648; <u>Commonweal</u>, 2/17/56, p. 516; <u>Look</u>, 2/21/56, p. 103-4; <u>Nation</u>, 2/11/56, p. 126; <u>Saturday Review</u>, 2/25/56, p. 27; <u>Scholastic</u>, 2/9/56, p. 39; <u>Time</u>, 3/19/56, p. 108

F37.   *BACKLASH*   (83 min., Color)

Universal, 1956
Producer: Aaron Rosenberg
Director: John Sturges
Screenplay: Borden Chase
Based on the novel by: Frank Gruber

Cast: Richard Widmark (*Jim Slater*), Donna Reed (*Karyl Orton*), John McIntire (*Jim Bonniwell*), William Campbell (*Johnny Cool*), Barton MacLane (*Sergeant Lake*), Harry Morgan (*Tony Welker*), Bob Wilke (*Jeff Welker*), Edward Platt (*Sheriff George Marson*)

Synopsis: Jim Slater and Karyl Orton team up to uncover the truth about an Apache raid in which five men were killed and $60,000 in gold was stolen by a sixth man who apparently sold his friends out to the attacking Indians. Slater is only looking for information regarding his father, whom he hopes was one of the men killed by the Indians, not the one who ran off with the gold. Karyl Orton, whose husband was one of the unlucky five, is searching for the gold. Six months later, they discover Slater's father, Jim Bonniwell, alive and the head of a rustling empire founded by the stolen gold. The ruthless Bonniwell is killed by ranchers in the end. Karyl doesn't get the gold, but she does get the man- Slater- with whom she has fallen in love along the way.

Review excerpts: To this "regulation western drama" Donna Reed and Richard Widmark add "name value" as per the review in <u>Variety</u> (3/7/56). "Miss Reed also handles her role well, that of a girl who hasn't always been what a lady's supposed to be."

Milton Esterow of the <u>New York Times</u> (4/21/56, p. 11) assessed, "as Karyl, Donna Reed is cool (except with Mr. Widmark), elegant and slightly bored. You can't blame her."

Additional reviews: <u>Commonweal</u>, 4/13/56, p. 49

F38.   *BEYOND MOMBASA* (U.K.)   (90 min., Color)

Columbia/Hemisphere, 1956
Producer: Tony Owen
Director: George Marshall

Screenplay: Richard English, Gene Levitt
Based on novel "The Mark of the Leopard" by: James Eastwood

Cast: Cornel Wilde (*Matt Campbell*), Donna Reed (*Ann Wilson*), Leo Genn (*Ralph Hoyt*), Ron Randell (*Elliott Hastings*), Christopher Lee (*Gil Rossi*), Dan Jackson (*Ketimi*), Eddie Calvert (*Trumpet player*), Bartholomew Sketch (*Native Boss*)

Synopsis: Matt Campbell travels to Kenya to help his brother who has discovered a uranium mine. He is informed upon his arrival that his brother has been murdered by "The Leopard Men," a bizarre African cult. Believing that his brother's death was in truth linked to his uranium discovery, Campbell sets out to find the mine. Ralph Hoyt, a seemingly gentle missionary who accompanies Campbell on the expedition, is revealed as the murderer only after a few more murders and attempts on Campbell's life. He committed the murders to prevent the mine from being reopened, and faked the "leopard men's" trademark claw marks on the bodies as a ploy to shift suspicion. The film's romantic conflict is supplied by Donna Reed as Ann Wilson, the missionary's niece who is initially repelled by Campbell's apparently avaricious motives. She later has a change of heart and the pair unite.

Review excerpts: The New York Times' review by Bosley Crowther (5/31/57, p. 14) termed the film a "routine African adventure" whose stars (Wilde, Reed, Genn and Randell) all "act in ordinary fashion for what is an ordinary film."

Variety's (10/17/56) reviewer observed "Donna Reed almost douses her Hollywood grooming to roam the wilds and find romance with the man she at first despises" in this "good stereotyped action picture."

Additional Reviews: Commonweal, 5/31/57, p. 232; National Parent-Teacher, 4/57, p. 37; Time, 6/24/57, p. 86

See also: "Star Ends Safari" (B65) relates some of Donna's experiences during the filming of "Beyond Mombasa" in East Africa.

Note: This was the first and last of her husband's films in which Donna appeared.

F39.   *THE WHOLE TRUTH*   (84 min., B/W)

Columbia Pictures, 1958
Producer: Jack Clayton
Director: John Guillermin
Screenplay: Jonathan Latimer
Based on play by: Philip Mackie

Cast: Stewart Granger (*Max Paulton*), Donna Reed (*Carol Paulton*), George Sanders (*Carliss*), Gianna Maria Canale (*Gina Bertini*), Michael Shillo (*Inspector Simon*), Richard Molinas (*Gilbert*)

Synopsis: Max Paulton is a movie producer who is bored in his marriage and has an affair with Gina, a temperamental actress who is working for him. He soon tires of the affair and decides to stay with his wife. Soon after their stormy parting, Gina is murdered, and Max becomes the prime suspect. After a few intriguing plot twists, Gina's unscrupulous husband Carliss is revealed as the murderer by Carol Paulton, who stuck by her husband through all.

Review excerpts: Variety (8/6/58) called the film "a routine effort which is unlikely to create outstanding interest." Donna Reed, one of the three marquee names which "should insure it satisfactory bookings on both sides of the Atlantic," is said to have "little to do but look decorative." The remainder of the cast and the director are given mild praise, with highest accolades going to Canale.

F40.   PEPE   (195 min., Color)

Columbia Pictures/George Sidney, 1960
Producer: Jacques Gelman
Director: George Sidney
Screenplay: Dorothy Kingsley and Claude Binyon
Based on story by: Leonard Spigelgass & Sonya Levien

Cast: Cantinflas (*Pepe*), Dan Dailey (*Ted Holt*), Shirley Jones (*Suzie Murphy*), Carlos Montalban (*Auctioneer*), Vicki Trickett (*Lupita*), Matt Mattox (*Dancer*), William Demarest (*Studio Gateman*), Michael Callan, Maurice Chevalier, Bing Crosby, Richard Conte, Bobby Darin, Sammy Davis, Jr., Jimmy Durante, Zsa Zsa Gabor, Judy Garland, Greer Garson, Hedda Hopper, Joey Bishop, Peter Lawford, Janet Leigh, Jack Lemmon, Dean Martin, Jay North, Kim Novak, Andre' Previn, Donna Reed, Debbie Reynolds, Edward G. Robinson, Frank Sinatra (*Themselves*)

Synopsis: Mexican peasant Pepe migrates to Hollywood when the stallion he loves and has cared for is sold to a movie producer. Pepe persuades Ted Holt, the animal's new owner, to let him stay and continue to care for it. He meets and falls in love with waitress Suzie Murphy, who loves Holt instead. Holt, whose excessive drinking is ruining his career, sells the horse for money to complete a film. Once again, Pepe is separated from his horse, a loss he takes harder than his loss of Suzie to Holt. When the horse's new owner, a movie mogul, wants to buy Holt's film, the producer demands the return of the horse to Pepe, and at long last Pepe and pal are reunited. During the course of the film, Pepe encounters dozens of Hollywood stars in cameo appearances.

Review excerpts: Rated overlong and oversized by the
New York Times (12/22/60, p. 18), whose reviewer
Bosley Crowther summed "George Sidney has produced
and directed (this film) about as tastelessly as it
could have been done."

Variety's (12/21/60, p. 6) reviewer was much less
harsh, citing the excessive running time as one of
the only drawbacks of this film, which has a "wealth
of entertainment."

Additional reviews: New Yorker, 12/31/60, p. 50;
Newsweek, 1/2/61, p. 66; Time, 1/2/61, p. 49

Note: As Donna performed only a brief cameo
appearance, she is not mentioned in the film's
reviews.

Roles Donna Didn't Play

The following is a brief list of films which are often mistakenly credited to Donna Reed.

CRY HAVOC (1943, MGM, 97 min., B/W)
Cast: Margaret Sullavan, Joan Blondell, Ann Sothern, Fay Bainter, Marsha Hunt, Ella Raines, Dorothy Morris, Connie Gilchrist
The role Donna was up for went to Dorothy Morris.

DEEP IN MY HEART (1954, MGM, 132 min., Color)
early title- THIS IS MY LOVE
Cast: Jose Ferrer, Merle Oberon, Paul Henreid, Walter Pidgeon, Helen Traubel, Doe Avedon, Tamara Toumanova
Was signed to play the wife of Sigmund Romberg in this musical biography of the composer. Doe Avedon played the role.

MRS. PARKINGTON (1944, MGM, 124 min., B/W)
Cast: Greer Garson, Walter Pidgeon, Edward Arnold, Frances Rafferty, Agnes Moorehead, Selena Royle
Donna was up for the role of Jane Stilham, but the part went to Frances Rafferty.

RIDE LONESOME (1959, Columbia, 73 min., B/W)
Cast: Randolph Scott, Karen Steele, Pernell Roberts, James Best, Lee Van Cleef

THE STRATTON STORY (1949, MGM, 106 min., B/W)
Cast: James Stewart, June Allyson, Frank Morgan, Agnes Moorehead, Bill Williams
Donna was cast opposite Van Johnson, but Johnson was suddenly replaced by Jimmy Stewart. Donna was thrilled to be working with Stewart again, but after the poor box office performance of It's A Wonderful Life, the producers didn't want to re-team Stewart and Reed and she was replaced by June Allyson.

TENDER FLESH   (1976, 85 min., Color)
WELCOME TO ARROW BEACH   (1973, 99 min., Color)
YELLOW-HEADED SUMMER
Cast: Laurence Harvey, Joanna Pettet, Stuart Whitman, John
Ireland, Gloria Leroy

In 1972 it was reported that Donna Reed and Walter Pidgeon
would be among the stars of Yellow-Headed Summer. When it
was finally released in 1973 as Welcome to Arrow Beach,
neither star was in the cast. Yet the film still appears on
many Reed filmographies.   Plot concerned a brother and
sister who have a fondness for human flesh, and it was
released again in 1976 under the title Tender Flesh.

Donna with her television family: Paul Petersen, Carl Betz, and Shelley Fabares. "The Donna Reed Show" ran for eight seasons on ABC (1958-1966).

Donna Reed in the mid-1980s.

Television Appearances

T1.   *1953 ACADEMY AWARDS*   (3/25/54, NBC, 2 hours+)

The nominations for Best Supporting Actress were: Grace Kelly for Mogambo, Geraldine Page for Hondo, Majorie Rambeau for Torch Song, Thelma Ritter for Pickup on South Street, and Donna Reed for From Here to Eternity. The envelope please...

When Donna Reed's name was announced by Walter Brennan, she sprinted down the aisle. Later she said "I ran? I don't believe it!" (see B261)

The ceremony was telecast live from the RKO Pantages Theatre in Hollywood (See A2).

T2.   *FORD TELEVISION THEATRE*   (12/16/54, NBC, 30 min.)
Episode- "Portrait of Lydia"

Two art students meet on a voyage to France, where they both plan to study. Later, in Paris, they both settle at Mama Michele's boarding house and their friendship turns to love. Written by Robert Smith and Berish Rubin.

Cast
Donna Reed (*Lydia Campbell*), Robert Horton (*Greg Howell*), Nan Boardman (*Mama Michele*), Jonathan Hale (*Judge Tamberg*)

T3.   *1954 ACADEMY AWARDS*   (3/30/55, NBC, 90 min.)

Donna Reed presented the Best Supporting Actor award to Edmond O'Brien for The Barefoot Contessa, and Frank Sinatra, the previous year's Supporting Actor winner presented the Best Supporting Actress award.

Telecast live from the RKO Pantages Theatre in Hollywood (see B88).

T4.   *GENERAL ELECTRIC THEATER*   (2/24/57, CBS, 60 min.)
      Episode- "Flight From Tormendero"

      During World War II, a ship's captain picked up the
      survivors of a torpedoed ship. Among those rescued
      were a pretty Eurasian girl and a sinister looking
      man. The Captain marries the man and woman, then
      after the war calls on them in their Meditteranean
      home. He finds the woman is being held virtually a
      prisoner on the island.

      Cast
      Donna Reed (*Rayna*), Helmut Dantine (*Manson*), George
      Macready (*Clive*)

      See also: Donna called this "the worst thing I've
      ever done" in a TV Guide interview the following year
      (See B64).

T5.   *SUSPICION*   (10/14/57, NBC, 60 min.)
      Episode- "The Other Side of the Curtain"

      A woman is troubled by a recurring dream about a dark
      hallway and a curtain at the end of it. Finally, she
      seeks counsel from a physchiatrist. Together she and
      the doctor try to discover what lies beyond the
      curtain, but in doing so they arouse suspicions as to
      the mysterious death of her husband's first wife.
      Adapted by James P. Cavanaugh from the mystery novel
      by Helen McCoy.

      Cast
      Donna Reed (*Letty Jason*), Jeff Richards, Ainslie
      Pryor

T6.   *THIS IS YOUR LIFE*   (3/26/58, NBC, 30 min.)
      "This Is Your Life, Donna Reed"

      Ralph Edwards (*Host*), William Mullenger, Hazel
      Mullenger, Bill Mullenger, Keith Mullenger, Heidi
      (Lavonne) Mullenger, Karen Mullenger, Tony Owen,
      Buddy Adler, Dr. Edward R. Tompkins, others (*Guests*)

      Donna believed she was to be a guest in a surprise
      tribute to producer Harry Joe Brown, but she was the
      one surprised instead. For this broadcast, Donna's
      entire family was reunited along with some old
      friends, teachers and others from her past.

T7.   *THE DONNA REED SHOW* (9/24/58 - 9/3/66, ABC, 30 min.)
      274 episodes

      Donna starred in this situation comedy centering on
      the Stone family of Hilldale. Donna Stone was the
      role model for wives and mothers nationwide, as they
      watched her capably manage her household and children
      each week. As the wife of a pediatrician, she was

always having to put up with her husband's long hours and the demands made by patients. As the mother of two teenagers, and adoptive mother of a younger child, she dealt with sparring siblings, broken hearts and broken toys with equal proficiency.

Syndication of "The Donna Reed Show" has given rise to a whole new generation of fans, and millions of viewers are discovering or re-discovering the Donna Reed Legend on national cable station Nickelodeon. "Nick at Nite" currently airs "The Donna Reed Show" twice every day. As proof that Donna Reed is still the ultimate symbol of motherhood, Nickelodeon held a "Seven Day Donna-Thon," airing twenty episodes a day for an entire week in observance of Mother's Day, 1990 (May 7th through the 13th).

Cast
Donna Reed (*Donna Stone*), Carl Betz (*Dr. Alex Stone*), Shelley Fabares (*Mary Stone*), Paul Petersen (*Jeff Stone*), Patty Petersen (*Trisha Stone*), Bob Crane (*Dr. Dave Kelsey*), Ann McCrea (*Midge Kelsey*), Darryl Richard (*Smitty*)

Created by: William Roberts
Producers: Tony Owen, William Roberts

Review excerpts: Variety (10/1/58) deemed the series a "pleasant situation comedy" adding "it has a good plus in pert, likeable Miss Reed."

Another positive vote from Variety appeared on 11/26/58: "delightful family show with deft touches of humor. But there's little audience left after Milton Berle and "The Millionaire" claim theirs."

However, the Variety reviewer who viewed the episode titled "Weekend", reported in the 9/21/60 issue that it was "almost too pollyanaish to be believed."

Related articles:
"Carl Betz has proved his ability on 'The Donna Reed Show' and off." TV Guide, June 29, 1963, p. 15-17
DeBlois, F. "The Donna Reed Show." (Review) TV Guide, February 14, 1959, p. 26
"Man, Is He Far Out!: Paul Petersen of 'The Donna Reed Show' gets his kicks on the trampoline." TV Guide, July 22, 1961, p. 21-22
"The Many Sins of Shelley Fabares." TV Guide, June 18, 1960, p. 24-26
Parsons, Louella O. "Unspoiled Shelley." New York Journal-American, October 18, 1964.
TV Guide, August 1, 1964, p. 8-9. (Picture feature on Paul Petersen and sister Patty.)

See also: Bibliography sections 1950s and 1960s contain numerous articles concerning the series.

An Episode Guide to "The Donna Reed Show" follows this section.

T8.   *1962 ACADEMY AWARDS*   (4/8/63, ABC, 2 hours+)

Donna Reed presented the Cinematography award; Frank
Sinatra was host.   Telecast live   from the Santa
Monica Civic Auditorium in California.

T9.   *1963 ACADEMY AWARDS*   (4/13/64, ABC, 3 hours)

Donna Reed presented the Costume Design award. Jack
Lemmon was the emcee.   Telecast live from the Santa
Monica Civic Auditorium in California.

T10.   *THE BEST PLACE TO BE*   (5/27-28/79, NBC, 4 hours)
A Ross Hunter Productions television film.

When Sheila Callahan's husband dies suddenly, she
must rebuild her life alone.   Her situation is
complicated by a hippie   daughter, a rebellious
teenage son and an ill-fated love affair with a
younger man- and then she finds real love with a
former suitor.

Cast
Donna Reed (*Sheila Callahan*), Efrem Zimbalist Jr.
(*Bill Reardon*), Mildred Dunnock (*Rose Price*), Betty
White (*Sally Cantrell*), John Phillip Law (*Dr. Gary
Mancini*), Stephanie Zimbalist (*Maryanne Callahan*),
Michael Shannon (*Patrick Callahan*), Gregory Harrison
(*Rick Jawlosky*), Timothy Hutton (*Tommy Callahan*),
Lloyd Bochner (*Bob Stockwood*)

Producers: Ross Hunter, Jacque Mapes
Director: David Miller
Writer: Stanford Whitmore
Based on the novel by: Helen Van Slyke

Review excerpts: Kay Gardella for the New York Daily
News (5/25/79), remarked that Donna Reed "doesn't
look as if she has aged one year" in this "super
glossy" production (see B145).

Less complimentary was Howard Rosenberg's Los Angeles
Times (5/26/79) piece, which claimed "anyplace else
is 'Best Place to Be'" (see B154).

Variety's (5/25/79) reviewer opined "Reed works her
silly role for all its worth, which is little.
Awkward scenes abound."

See also: Donna discussed at length her reasons for
doing this project in Robert Osborne's column in the
Hollywood Reporter (B151).

T11.   *AFI SALUTE TO FRANK CAPRA*   (4/4/82, CBS, 90 min.)

On March 4, 1982, the American Film Institute held a
testimonial in Beverly Hills to present director

Frank Capra with their Life Achievement Award. James Stewart was the host. Guests included Bette Davis, Charlton Heston, Claudette Colbert, Donna Reed, Fred MacMurray, and Bob Hope. The tribute was broadcast with clips from Capra films.

T12.   *DEADLY LESSONS*   (3/7/83, ABC, 2 hours)
       early title- "The Girls of Starkwater Hall"

The girls of Starkwater Hall are being systematically murdered one by one. In addition to the murderer's identity, a number of other secrets are uncovered at the exclusive girl's prep school. The strict headmistress, Miss Wade, is having an affair with one of the prime suspects, a younger riding instructor. After half a dozen girls are killed it is discovered that the murders are related to a secret in Miss Wade's past.

Cast
Donna Reed (*Miss Wade*), Larry Wilcox (*Detective Russ Kemper*), David Ackroyd (*John Ferrar*), Diane Franklin (*Stefanie Aggiston*), Ally Sheedy (*Marita Armstrong*), Donald Hotton (*Robert Hartigan*), Renee Jones (*Cally*), Deena Freeman (*Lauren Peele*), Vicki Kriegler (*Shama*), Nancy Cartwright (*Libby Dean*), Krista Errickson (*Tember*), Rick Rossovich (*Craig*)

Producer: Leonard Goldberg, Deborah Aal, Ervin Zavada
Director: William Wiard
Writer: Jennifer A. Miller

See also: "It wasn't very well done," Donna said of "Deadly Lessons" in a 1984 TV Guide article, "but I played a cold, authoritarian head of a girl's school, and it was a stretch for me" (see B163).

T13.   *THE LOVE BOAT*   (2/4/84, ABC, 2 hours)
       Segment- "Polly's Poker Palace"

This two hour special took the "Love Boat" to Hong Kong. As with each episode of the series, several stories concerning the passengers and crew are interwoven. The segment Donna appeared in concerned a senator- played by Efrem Zimbalist, Jr.- who romances a woman until he learns the nature of her business in port.

Regular Cast
Gavin MacLeod, Lauren Tewes, Bernie Kopell, Fred Grandy, Ted Lange, Jill Whelan

Guest Cast
Donna Reed, Efram Zimbalist, Jr., Gene Kelly, Brenda Vacarro, Yvette Mimieux, Leigh McCloskey, Lee Yeary, Jr., Pamela Hensley, Ben Murphy, Noel Harrison

T14.   *DALLAS*   (11/9/84 - 1985, CBS)

On November 9, 1984, Donna Reed stepped into the role
of Miss Ellie, the matriarch of the powerful Ewing
family of Dallas. The role had been originated by
Barbara Bel Geddes, who left due to illness. Donna's
characterization was different, but she was gaining
acceptance of critics and viewers alike. On April
11, 1985, she learned that "Dallas" producers were
planning to bring Bel Geddes back to the role. Donna
was not about to step aside gracefully. She had two
years left on her contract, and had enjoyed working
on the series. Angered at producers, and hurt by
unkind media headlines, Donna fought back. She sued
Lorimar, the producers of "Dallas" for $7 million
dollars, and tried to stop production of all scenes
involving the Miss Ellie character until the matter
was resolved. She was denied an injunction to halt
production, but was eventually awarded $1.25 million
in damages.

Cast
Larry Hagman (*J.R. Ewing*), Patrick Duffy (*Bobby
Ewing*), Donna Reed (*Eleanor "Miss Ellie" Ewing*),
Linda Gray (*Sue Ellen Ewing*), Victoria Principal
(*Pamela Ewing*), Howard Keel (*Clayton Farlow*), Ken
Kercheval (*Cliff Barnes*)

Producers: Philip Capice, Lee Rich, Leonard Katzman
Directors: Victor French, Patrick Duffy, Larry
Hagman, Leonard Katzman, Vincent McEveety
Writers: Leonard Katzman, Arthur Bernard Lewis,
Howard Lakin, Loraine Despres
Creator: David Jacobs

See: B156, B157, B160-168, B170-180, B182, B185-190
for articles about "Dallas."

"The Donna Reed Show"
Episode Guide

The following is a chronological listing of each of the 274 episodes of "The Donna Reed Show." Title and air date are followed by writer "W," director "D" and guest star "GS" credits (also Teleplay "T" and Story by "S" where applicable), and a brief plot synopsis. Information is sparse for some non-syndicated episodes.

DR1. "Weekend Trip"   9/24/58
W: Phil Leslie   D: Andrew McCullough
GS: Jack Kelk (*Dr. Boland*), Howard Wendell (*George Heiser*), Alice Reinheart (*Mrs. Barclay*), Louise Lewis (*Mrs. Whitman*), Hugh Corcoran (*Eddie*)
Donna and Alex experience difficulties getting away with the kids for the weekend.

DR2. "Pardon My Gloves"   10/1/58
W: Alan Lipscott & Bob Fisher   D: Oscar Rudolph
GS: Mary Shipp (*Lydia Langley*), Kim Charney (*Chunky Langley*)
When a boy criticizes Donna's acting in a local play, Jeff fights him and gets a black eye. Donna then tries to teach Jeff to box- from a book!

DR3. "The Hike"   10/8/58
W: Jay Sommers & Don Nelson   D: Oscar Rudolph
GS: Scott Morrow (*Peewee*), Ricky Klein (*1st Boy*), Stephen Pearson (*2nd Boy*), Alan Aaronson (*3rd Boy*), Martin Smith (*Ranger*)
Donna wants to prove capable as an "outdoorsman," so she fills in for Alex on a camping trip with Jeff and his friends.

DR4. "The Male Ego"   10/15/58
W: Nate Monaster   D: Oscar Rudolph
GS: Lawrence Dobkin (*Dr. Winfield Graham*), Alvy Moore (*Hank*), Jack Straw (*Salesman*), Sid Tomack (*Mac*)
Alex feels threatened when he feels that Donna has become the head of the household.

DR5.   **"The Football Uniform"**   10/22/58
W: William Cowley & Peggy Chantler   D: Oscar Rudolph
GS: Hugh Corcoran (*Eddie Barclay*), Robert McKenny
(*Tom Ellis*)
Unaware of who the other bidders are, Jeff, Alex and
Donna each try to outbid the rest for a football
uniform for Jeff.

DR6.   **"The Foundling"**   10/29/58
W: John Whedon   D: Oscar Rudolph
GS: Paul Picerni (*Tony, the Milkman*), Fintan Meyler
(*Kathleen*), Don Hildreth (*Policeman*)
The Stones find a baby on their doorstep and try to
find its mother.

DR7.   **"The Three Part Mother"**   11/5/58
W: Nate Monaster   D: Oscar Rudolph
GS: Ross Elliott (*Woody Graham*)
Busy Donna has obligations to attend three different
functions on the same night.

DR8.   **"Change Partners and Dance"**   11/12/58
W: William Roberts   D: James Kern
GS: Jimmy Hawkins (*George Haskell*), Dena Bliss
(*Betty*)
Donna teaches Mary's prom date how to dance, and the
boy develops a crush on Donna.

DR9.   **"Dough Re Mi"**   11/19/58
W: Bob Fisher & Alan Lipscott   D: Oscar Rudolph
GS: Mary Shipp (*Lydia Langley*), Roger Til (*Anton
Duval*), Reba Waters (*Antoinette Duval*)
Donna and Jeff both get involved in fund raising
ventures.

DR10.   **"Guest in the House"**   11/26/58
W: John Whedon   D: Oscar Rudolph
GS: Charles Herbert (*David Barker*), John Bryant
(*Major Barker*), Stephen Courtleigh (*Colonel
Woodward*), John Reach (*Police Officer*)
A patient of Dr. Stone's runs away from military
school and ends up spending Thanksgiving weekend with
the Stones. The disobedient boy gives the family a
tough time, until Donna breaks through to him.

DR11.   **"The Baby Contest"**   12/3/58
W: William Cowley & Peggy Chantler D: Oscar Rudolph
GS: Virginia Christine (*Margaret*), Anne Whitfield
(*Helen Cooper*), Ruth Terry (*Ruth Sterling*), Dorothy
Morris (*Shirley Watson*), Gerry Lock (*Myra Robinson*)
Alex is named judge in a baby beauty contest run by
Donna's club.

DR12.   **"The Beaded Bag"**   12/10/58
W: Nate Monaster   D: Oscar Rudolph
GS: Mary Treen (*Miss Winters*), Angela Greene (*Patsy
Cole*), Rickie Sorensen (*Bobby Cole*), Robert Nash
(*Man*)
Donna schemes to get Alex to buy her an expensive
beaded handbag.

DR13. **"The Busy Body"** 12/17/58
T: Henry Sharp, Kay Leonard & Jess Carneol
S: Kay Leonard & Jess Carneol   D: Oscar Rudolph
GS: Rhys Williams (*Uncle Fred*), Ann Doran (*Mrs. Adams*), Irving Bacon (*Mayor Webster*)
Donna's uncle comes for a visit, and the more he tries to help everyone, the more he messes things up.

DR14. **"A Very Merry Christmas"** 12/24/58
W: Nate Monaster   D: Oscar Rudolph
GS: Buster Keaton (*Charlie*), Butler Hixson (*Dr. Florey*), Murray Alper (*Joe*)
Fed up with the commercialization of Christmas, Donna finds the true holiday spirit helping the janitor at the hospital put together a party for the children.

DR15. **"Mary's Double Date"** 12/31/58
W: Alan Lipscott & Bob Fisher   D: Oscar Rudolph
GS: Buzz Martin (*Charlie*), Bobby Burgess (*Ernie*), Tom Brandt (*Phil*)
Mary has to choose between two football players for a date to the school prom.

DR16. **"Jeff's Double Life"** 1/7/59
W: Bill Manhoff   D: Oscar Rudolph
GS: Kathleen Freeman (*Mrs. Wilgus*), Peter Adams (*Dr. Barry*)
Jeff hurts his arm while on a joyride with a friend. In order to esape trouble, Jeff gives a different name when he goes to see a doctor.

DR17. **"Nothing But the Truth"** 1/21/59
W: John Whedon   D: Oscar Rudolph
GS: Charles Herbert (*David Barker*), Gregory Irvin (*Mousie Myers*), Jimmy Fields (*Snyder*)
David Barker, the boy from a previous episode, returns to spend his birthday with the Stones.

DR18. **"It's the Principle of the Thing"** 1/14/59
W: Jerry Davis & Tom August   D: Oscar Rudolph
GS: Hans Conreid (*Mr. Popkin*), Richard Deacon (*Mr. Johnson*), Bobby Crawford (*Joey*), David McMahon (*Cop*)
Donna helps a poor man earn enough money to pay for his son's medical treatment.

DR19. **"Jeff vs. Mary"** 1/28/59
T: Alan Lipscott, Bob Fisher & Henry Sharp
S: Alan Lipscott & Bob Fisher   D: Oscar Rudolph
GS: Stephen Pearson (*Zachary Blake*), Jack Kelk (*Dr. Boland*), Pat McCaffrie (*Electrician*)
Jeff believes his parents love Mary more than him.

DR20. **"Have Fun"** 1/3/59
W: John Whedon   D: Oscar Rudolph
GS: George Hamilton (*Herbie Shields*), Sherwood Price (*Dr. Hooper*), Arthur Lovejoy (*Headwaiter*)
Donna and Alex recall different versions of their first date. Since Mary's first date with Herbie Shields went as badly as Alex and Donna's first date did, everyone is sure things will work out.

DR21. **"Donna Plays Cupid"**   2/11/59
       T: Henry Sharp, Bob Fisher & Alan Lipscott
       S: Bob Fisher & Alan Lipscott   D: Oscar Rudolph
       GS: Jack Kelk (*Bo*), Susan Dorn (*Ceil Pennington*), Hal
       Baylor (*Herbie Armbruster*), Joanna Lee (*Connie*)
       Donna tries to find a perfect wife for Dr. Boland.

DR22. **"Love Thy Neighbor"**   2/18/59
       W: Nate Monaster   D: Oscar Rudolph
       GS: Kathleen Freeman (*Mrs. Wilgus*), Howard McNear
       (*Mr. Wilgus*), Maudie Prickett (*Miss Sanders*), Cosmo
       Sardo (*Maitre'D*)
       Donna and Alex are invited to their neighbors'
       anniversary party and end up trying to reunite the
       fighting couple.

DR23. **"Report Card"**   2/25/59
       W: Nate Monaster   D: Oscar Rudolph
       GS: Harvey Grant (*Philip*), Ann Doran (*Mrs. Adams*),
       Stephen Pearson   (*Zachary*),   Irene   Vernon (*Miss
       Standish*)
       Donna is dismayed when Jeff brings home an all "C"
       report card. She thinks he can do better.

DR24. **"Boys Will Be Boys"**   3/4/59
       W: John Whedon   D: Oscar Rudolph
       GS: Charles Herbert (*David Barker*), John Harmon
       (*Rat*), Ric Roman (*Gangster*), Darlene Fields (*Moll*),
       Carleton Young (*Major Ryan*)
       David Barker returns again. His father brings the boy
       to Dr. Stone for a rabies shot.

DR25. **"The Ideal Wife"**   3/11/59
       W: Nate Monaster   D: Oscar Rudolph
       GS: Sid Tomack (*Mac*), Keith Richards (*Dr. Lester
       Brock*), Frances Robinson (*Ellen Marcy*), Don Harvey
       (*Dr. Harry Marcy*), Gerry Lock (*Kate Brock*)
       Fed up with being taken for granted, Donna lashes out
       at Alex, the kids- and the cleaning man.

DR26. **"Mary's Campaign"**   3/18/59
       GS: Gigi Perreau
       Mary gets carried away by her nomination as class
       secretary, and she tries to change her family to fit
       her campaign.

DR27. **"The Flowered Print Dress"**   3/25/59
       W: Nate Monaster   D: Oscar Rudolph
       GS: Addison Richards (*Dr. Butler*), Lillian Bronson
       (*Mrs. Butler*), Olive Sturgess (*Carol Berke*), Keith
       Vincent (*Jim Berke*)
       After spending an evening with a younger couple,
       Donna and Alex question whether or not the life has
       gone out of their marriage.

DR28. **"April Fool"**   4/1/59
       W: Jerry Davis & Tom August   D: Oscar Rudolph
       GS: James Darren (*Buzz Berry*), Jesse White (*Lou
       Vance*), Ted Knight (*Phil Martin*), Nancy Randall
       (*Alice*), Doreen Tracy (*Flo*), Melinda Plowman (*Sue*)

A singing idol stays with the Stones when he comes down with the measles. His overbearing agent may wear out his welcome.

DR29. **"The Parting of the Ways"** 4/8/59
W: John Whedon D: Oscar Rudolph
GS: Mary Lawrence (*Myra Keppler*), Melinda Plowman (*Babs Keppler*), Pat McCaffrie (*Jack Keppler*)
Mary's friend thinks her parents are breaking up and comes to Mary for advice. Mary overhears Donna and Alex arguing, and also jumps to the wrong conclusion.

DR30. **"The Hero"** 4/15/59
T: John Whedon S: Nate Monaster D: Oscar Rudolph
GS: Ben Gage (*Biff Jameson*), Jimmy Hawkins (*George Haskell*), Tom Palmer (*Harry*), Gordon Gebert (*Stanley*)
Alex's college roommate and football hero visits and gets a lesson on the important things in life.

DR31. **"Do You Trust Your Child?"** 4/22/59
W: Jerry Davis & Tom August D: Oscar Rudolph
GS: Richard Tyler (*Leonard*), Florida Friebus (*Helen Brooks*), Jymme Shore (*Nancy*)
Donna becomes known as an "expert" in dealing with children, but the advice changes when the children are her own.

DR32. **"The Grateful Patient"** 4/29/59
W: Nate Monaster D: Oscar Rudolph
GS: Kathleen Freeman (*Mrs. Wilgus*), Howard McNear (*Mr. Wilgus*), Jack Straw (*Mr. Alexander*)
A patient's husband promises Alex a big return on his investment in a syndicate, and the family starts spending the money before they get it.

DR33. **"The Testimonial"** 5/6/59
W: Nate Monaster D: Oscar Rudolph
GS: James Bell (*Dr. Jason*), Olive Blakeney (*Mrs. Jason*), Tommy Andre (*Willie*), Harry Cheshire (*Mayor*), Bruce Hayes (*Wagner*), Stephen Roberts (*Mr. Herman*)
When Donna realizes that a retiring doctor doesn't really want to retire, she turns his farewell dinner into a testimonial.

DR34. **"Miss Lovelace Comes to Tea"** 5/13/59
W: Henry Sharp D: Oscar Rudolph
GS: Estelle Winwood (*Miss Lovelace*), Margaret Dumont (*Mrs. Westcott Trilling*), Esther Dale (*Mrs.Arbogast*), Elizabeth Talbot-Martin (*Matron*)
The Stones hire a housekeeper so that Donna can have more time for her charity work. In short time, Donna and the housekeeper trade jobs.

DR35. **"Tomorrow Comes Too Soon"** 5/20/59
W: Nate Monaster D: Oscar Rudolph
GS: Harry Ellerbe (*Phil*), Joan Tompkins (*Patty*), Gary Troy (*Jim*)
Time away from Mary and Jeff makes Donna and Alex realize how much they'll miss the kids when they leave home.

DR36. "Advice to Young Lovers"   5/27/59
       W: John Whedon   D: Oscar Rudolph
       GS: Jimmy Hawkins (*George*), Melinda Plowman (*Babs*)
       While helping Mary to win back George, Donna recalls
       how she got Alex to propose to her.

DR37. "Operation Deadbeat"   6/3/59
       W: Si Rose & Seaman Jacobs   D: Oscar Rudolph
       GS: Alan Reed (*Mr. Finsterwald*), William Keene (*Mr.
       McDonnell*), H. Perry Cook (*Mr. Folger*), Tony Miller
       (*Checker*)
       Jeff takes two part-time jobs in order to repay his
       debts.   Meanwhile, Donna tries to collect money
       Alex's patients owe him.

DR38. "That's Show Business"   9/9/59
       W: Jerry Davis & Tom August   D: Oscar Rudolph
       GS: Lee Aaker (*Kenny*), Herbert C. Lytton (*Mr. Cooper*)
       Mary and a painfully shy boy are teamed as dance
       partners in the school play.

DR39. "Sleep No More My Lady"   9/16/59
       W: Henry Sharp   D: Oscar Rudolph
       GS: Richard Gaines (*Dr. Elias Spaulding*), Helen
       Bennett (*Mrs. Spaulding*), Jean Paul King (*Dr.
       Brannan*)
       After a restless night and a long trip, Donna falls
       asleep in the middle of Alex's speech at a medical
       convention. Her attempts to explain herself to his
       colleagues only worsen the situation.

DR40. "A Penny Earned"   10/1/59
       W: Tom August   D: Oscar Rudolph
       GS: Irene Hervey (*Louise Collier*), Raymond Bailey
       (*George Collier*), Mary Carver (*Miss Robbins*), Jacques
       Scott (*Henri*), Christopher Essay (*Waiter*)
       Alex takes a "rate your wife quiz" in a magazine and
       gives Donna a perfect score. She resents getting 100%
       in thrift and threatens to go on a shopping spree.

DR41. "A Friend Indeed"   10/8/59
       W: Tom August   D: Oscar Rudolph
       GS: Ann Morriss (*Fran*), Doreen Lang (*Miss Ferguson*),
       Morris Lippert (*Doug*)
       Jeff takes the blame for some pranks pulled by one of
       his friends, but refuses to tell who he's protecting.

DR42. "The First Child"   10/15/59
       W: Nate Monaster   D: Oscar Rudolph
       GS: Alice Backes (*Mrs. Brandon*), Dave Willock (*Mr.
       Brandon*), Jack Bryan (*Manager*)
       A nervous couple with a newborn baby continually
       interrupt Alex and Donna with their worries and
       questions.

DR43. "Going Steady"   10/22/59
       W: Nate Monaster   D: Oscar Rudolph
       GS: Sherry Alberoni (*Meredith Penner*)
       Mary bribes Jeff to go to a girl's party so she can
       meet the girl's older brother.

DR44. **"The Neighborly Gesture"** 10/29/59
W: John Whedon   D: Oscar Rudolph
GS: Robert   Nichols (*Joe   Moody*),   Barbara   Eiler
(*Eleanor Moody*)
Jeff spends so much time with the new neighbors that
Alex becomes jealous.

DR45. **"Nothing Like a Good Book"** 11/5/59
W: John Whedon   D: Oscar Rudolph
GS: Mary Shipp (*Lydia Langley*), Frank Wilcox (*Bartley
Langley*), J. Edward McKinley (*Dr. Peabody*), Susan
Dorn (*Ceil Pennington*), Margie Liszt (*Vera Platt*),
Fred Kruger (*George*), Randy Preissman (*Christopher*)
Donna and Alex try to get their children interested
in literature.

DR46. **"Flowers for the Teacher"** 11/12/59
GS: Marion Ross (*Miss McGinnis*)
Jeff's new teacher fears she'll lose control of her
class, but her strict authority results in an
absentee problem.

DR47. **"All Mothers Worry"** 11/19/59
W: Nate Monaster   D: Oscar Rudolph
GS: William Schallert (*Bert Rose*), Ann Doran
(*Margaret Dorsey*), Harvey Grant (*Philip Dorsey*), and
the following members of the Los Angeles Rams: Sid
Gillman, Les Richter, Bill Wade, Don Burroughs, Bob
Kelley
A boy on Jeff's football team must resign because his
overprotective mother is afraid he'll get hurt. Alex
tries to teach her a lesson.

DR48. **"Jeff Joins a Club"** 11/26/59
W: Tom August   D: Oscar Rudolph
GS: Tony Haig (*Walter*), Scott Morrow (*Pee Wee*),
Stephen Pearson (*Zack*), Randy Preissman (*Robert*)
Jeff's hopes of joining a club are dashed when he has
to bring the new kid in town to the meeting.

DR49. **"The Punishment"** 12/3/59
W: Nate Monaster   D: Oscar Rudolph
GS: Robert Ellis (*Young Man*), Lenore Kingston (*Woman*)
Donna is forced to ground Mary and Jeff for
disobeying her, and she resents the fact that she is
always the one doling out punishment.

DR50. **"A Difference of Opinion"** 12/10/59
W: Nate Monaster   D: Ida Lupino
GS: Ann Rutherford (*Phyllis Baker*), Chet Stratton
(*Harry Baker*), Hal Smith (*Rod*), Holly Harris (*Elsie*),
Renny McEvoy (*Fred*), Alice Foote (*Joan*)
Donna and Alex try to hide their disputes from their
children when they learn the kids are embarassed by
the way their friends' parents fight.

DR51. **"The Homecoming Dance"** 12/17/59
W: John Whedon   D: Robert Ellis Miller
GS: Jay Strong (*Stan*), David DeHaven (*Dick*), Suzi
Carnell (*Betty Smith*), Tommy Ivo (*Herbie*)

Donna and Alex worry about Mary's blind date with a college boy. They allay their fears by driving Mary to the dance.

DR52. **"Lucky Girl"**   12/31/59
W: Nate Monaster   D: Oscar Rudolph
GS: Kristine Miller (*Betty Murdock*), Helen Conrad (*Woman*), Margie Liszt (*Beauty Operator*), Mona Knox (*Jane Lawrence*), Gerry Lock (*Helen*), Dorothy Kingston (*Dorothy Elliott*)
All the women in the neighborhood think Alex is such a wonderful guy that Donna begins to wish he were more like other stubborn husbands.

DR53. **"The Broken Spirit"**   1/7/60
W: Nate Monaster   D: Lawrence Dobkin
GS: Raymond Hatton (*Mr. Barnhill*), Ronald Anton (*Timmy*), Virginia Stefan (*Nurse*)
Jeff turns too-good-to-be-true when he believes himself responsible for an old man's accident.

DR54. **"The Secret"**   1/14/60
W: Norman Tokar   D: Nate Monaster
GS: Roberta Shore (*Carol*), Michael Vandever (*Matthew Morgan*), Tommy Ivo (*Herbie*)
Mary hides an engagement ring for her friend Carol, and when Donna finds it she thinks Mary is planning to elope.

DR55. **"The New Mother"**   1/21/60
W: John Whedon   D: Oscar Rudolph
GS: Charles Herbert (*David Barker*), John Bryant (*Major Barker*), Gregory Irvin (*Mousie*), Stephen Courtleigh (*Colonel Woodward*), Ina Victor (*Helen*)
David Barker runs away again and Jeff hides him in the basement. His father is remarrying but plans to leave the boy in military school.

DR56. **"Just a Housewife"**   1/28/60
W: Nate Monaster   D: Oscar Rudolph
GS: Constance Moore (*Doris*), Jerry Hausner (*Jerry Parker*), Elaine Riley (*Dorothy Burns*), Eileen Harley (*Joan Standish*), Lindsay Workman (*Jim*), Virginia Stefan (*Nurse*)
Donna is offended by a radio show host's treatment of women-- housewives in particular- and tries to raise his consciousness.

DR57. **"The Free Soul"**   2/4/60
W: David Adler   D: Norman Tokar
GS: Myron McCormick (*Dan*), Aline Towne (*Mrs. Sutton*), Charles Wagenheim (*Vendor*)
A friend of Jeff's grandfather influences Jeff to do what he wants to do and neglect responsibility.

DR58. **"The First Quarrel"**   2/11/60
W: Nate Monaster   D: Robert Ellis Miller
GS: Olive Sturgess (*Alice Burke*), Keith Vincent (*Jim Burke*), Kevin Burke (*Walter*), Duci de Kerekjarto (*Violinist*)

Alex gives advice to Jim, a friend who is fighting
with his wife. Donna gives conflicting advice to
Jim's wife, Alice. The couple finally reconciles
without interference from the Stones.

DR59. **"A Place to Go"** 2/18/60
W: John Whedon   D: Norman Tokar
GS: Stephen Wootton (*Wilbur*), Gerry Lock (*Myra
Keppler*), Ann Morriss (*Eleanor Moody*), Howard Wendell
(*George Heiser*), Lester Vail (*Matthew Sarples*)
Donna's club fixes up an old house for Jeff and his
friends to play in, but the boys aren't as interested
as they were when they weren't allowed inside it.

DR60. **"A Night to Howl"** 2/25/60
W: John Whedon   D: Lawrence Dobkin
GS: Mario Siletti (*Waiter*), Don Orlando (*Chef*), Tom
McKee (*Counterman*), Richard Reeves (*Construction
Worker*)
Convinced that they have fallen into a rut, Donna and
Alex spend a night on the town, but neither of them
is willing to admit they'd rather be home.

DR61. **"The Editorial"** 3/3/60
W: Nate Monaster   D: Lawrence Dobkin
GS: Alma Platt (*Mrs. Walters*), Mary Lou Kenworthy
(*Patty*), Andy Kirk (*Larry*), Michael Webber (*Mike*),
Larry Hart (*Rick*)
When Jeff's editorial on homework is yanked from the
school paper, he decides to distribute it himself.

DR62. **"The Gentle Dew"** 3/10/60
W: John Whedon   D: Norman Tokar
GS: Jan Stine (*Roger*), Arthur Hanson (*Ben Wiley*),
Aline Towne (*Kay Wiley*)
Mary fails to return home from a date on time, and
Alex decides the kids need more discipline.

DR63. **"The Fatal Leap"** 3/17/60
W: John Whedon   D: Andrew McCullough
GS: Florence MacMichael (*Madeleine Richards*), Jack
Albertson (*Jack Richards*), Charles Davis (*Moose
Edwards*), Sam Flint (*Dr. Wiggins*)
Donna is annoyed by Alex's eagerness to attend a
friend's bachelor party.

DR64. **"Perfect Pitch"** 3/24/60
W: Tom & Helen August   D: Norman Tokar
GS: Franco Corsaro (*Mr. Tocari*), Jerry Lawrence
(*Larry Waggner*), Tony Haig (*Greg*), Harry James
Donna pushes Jeff into taking trumpet lessons when
she learns he has perfect pitch. Unfortunately,
"perfect pitch" and musical talent don't always go
hand in hand.

DR65. **"Pickles for Charity"** 4/7/60
W: Nate Monaster   D: Norman Tokar
GS: William Newell (*Mr. Ross*), Tiger Fafara
(*Charlie*), Jean Cook (*1st Woman*), Jeanne Tatum (*2nd
Woman*), Fern Barry (*3rd Woman*), Helen Jay (*4th Woman*)

Everyone loves Donna's pickles, but when she tries to sell them to raise money, no one buys.

DR66.   **"Mary's Growing Pains"**   4/14/60
W: John Whedon   D: Lawrence Dobkin
GS: Jack Hilton (*Dr. Somers*), Jan Stine (*Roger*),
Abbagail Shelton (*Nurse*), Ann Seaton (*Older Nurse*)
Mary falls in love with a young intern and
misinterprets his kindness as romantic interest.

DR67.   **"Alex Runs the House"**   4/21/60
W: Tom & Helen August   D: Lawrence Dobkin
GS: Renee Godfrey (*Wilma*)
With Donna and Jeff away, Alex and Mary are left to
take care of themselves. Among other changes, Alex
decides dishes should only be done every four days.

DR68.   **"The Career Woman"**   4/28/60
W: Nate Monaster   D: Lawrence Dobkin
GS: Esther Williams (*Molly Duncan*), Richard Garland
(*David Anderson*), Don Burroughs (*Dr. Jim Folger*),
Janet Lord (*Saleswoman*), Morgan Jones (*Waiter*)
Donna's high school friend Molly, now a famous
designer, comes to Hilldale to see if she would be
happy married to a small town doctor.

DR69.   **"Jeff, the Financial Genius"**   5/5/60
W: Henry Sharp   D: Hy Averback
GS: Herb Vigran (*Mr. Sprague*), Marjorie Winters (*Mrs.
Pruitt*), Mike Montgomery (*Zack*), Mike Peters (*Alvin*)
Jeff repays his debts by swapping his belongings.

DR70.   **"Mary's Crusade"**   5/12/60
W: Nate Monaster   D: Lawrence Dobkin
GS: Melinda Byron (*Ellen*), Barbara Luddy (*Mrs.
Schiller*), Scooter Teague (*Don Morgan*), Carole Wells
(*Melanie*), Michael Eden (*Frank*), Don Edmonds (*Mort*),
Carl Crow (*Bert Singleton*)
Mary promises her plain looking friend that she won't
go to the dance unless they both get dates. She then
tries to transform the girl into a beauty.

DR71.   **"The First Time We Met"**   5/19/60
W: Nate Monaster   D: Robert Ellis Miller
GS: Bob Hastings (*Dr. Hank Landers*), Dorothy Kingston
(*Florence Kessler*), Kaye Elhardt (*Pat Archer*),
Lindsay Workman (*Dr. Kane*)
Donna tries to fix up a young doctor with a nurse.
Meanwhile, she and Alex can't agree on how they first
met and who arranged it.

DR72.   **"The Gossip"**   5/26/60
W: David Adler   D: Robert Ellis Miller
GS: Elisabeth Fraser (*Emily*), Maxine Cooper (*Kay*),
Gil Frye (*Ben Wiley*), Sheila Bromley (*Margaret*),
Almira Sessions (*Elsie*), Lindsay Workman (*Dr. Jim*)
Donna tells the town gossip that a friend is
expecting, and the news spreads fast. Soon another
rumor is circulating around Hilldale- that Donna and
Alex are having marital problems.

DR73. "Love's Sweet Awakening"   6/2/60
W: David Adler   D: Robert Ellis Miller
GS: Ralph Reed (Petey), Dan Tobin (George Handler),
Jeanne Bates (Ruth Handler), Carole Wells (Melanie)
The young man who grew up next door suddenly takes a
romantic interest in Mary, but she doesn't notice-
until her friend Melanie wants to date him.

DR74. "The Wedding Present"   6/9/60
W: Phil Sharp   D: Hy Averback
GS: Harriet MacGibbon (Mrs. Manning), Molly Dodd
(Louise Barnett), Tommy Farrell (Mr. Jason)
Donna is pressured into buying an antique and can't
bring herself to tell Alex.

DR75. "Cool Cat"   6/16/60
W: Jacqueline Trotte   D: Andrew McCullough
GS: Jimmy Hawkins (Jerry Hager), Marjorie Winters
(Ruth Morton), Roy Wright (Mr. Schultz)
A stray cat follows Jeff home, and later brings her
four kittens.

DR76. "Weekend"   9/15/60
W: Sam Adams   D: Andrew McCullough
GS: Parker Fennelly (Charlie), Mary Treen (Sunny
Cooper), Ed Stoddard (Man), Lorraine Miller (Woman)
The Stones vacation at a mountain resort and find the
accomodations aren't up to their expectations.

DR77. "The Mystery Woman"   9/22/60
W: Barbara Hammer   D: Norman Tokar
GS: Andrea King (Wanda Harmon), Tommy Ivo (Herbie),
Patti Brill (Hostess), Madge Blake (Woman #1), Gloria
Saunders (Woman #2)
A strange woman claims to be Donna's old friend, but
Donna can't remember her or find out who she is.

DR78. "Donna Decorates"   9/29/60
W: Seymour Friedman   D: Andrew McCullough
GS: Jay North (Dennis the Menace), Joseph Kearns (Mr.
Wilson), George Ives (John Coutts), George Cisar
(Dexter), Nick Nicholson (Plumber), Jerry Mann
(Painter #1), Paul Marco (Painter #2)
Donna redecorates the livingroom with some unwelcome
help from Dennis the Menace. Jay North and Joseph
Kearns from "Dennis the Menace" guest star.

DR79. "The Love Letter"   10/6/60
W: Tom & Helen August   D: Robert Ellis Miller
GS: Jay Novello (Nick Melinas), Maurice Manson (Mr.
Brown), Irene Vernon (Mrs. Brown), Peter Helm
(Danny), Nancy Ann De Carl (Peggy)
Jeff ghost-writes love letters for their Greek
handyman, but Donna thinks they're Jeff's.

DR80. "How the Other Half Lives"   10/20/60
W: John Whedon   D: James Sheldon
GS: Reba Waters (Ginny), John Graham (Mr. Currier)
After spending a weekend at a wealthy friend's house,
Mary is ashamed to invite her friend to the Stones.

DR81.   **"Alex's Twin"**   10/27/60
W: Nate Monaster   D: Jeffrey Hayden
GS: Jack Albertson (*Jack Richards*), Joe Gallison (*Jim Higgins*), Ray Baumann (*Elroy*), Cheerio Meredith (*Miss Graham*), Lindsay Workman (*Dr. Higgins*)
Mary dates a boy she believes is just like Alex must have been when he was younger. Alex is disturbed by the comparisons until the boy performs a heroic act.

DR82.   **"Worried Anyone?"**   11/3/60
W: Clifford Goldsmith   D: Robert Ellis Miller
GS: Jimmy Hawkins (*Scotty*), Robert N. Terry (*Mr. Simpson*)
Donna and Alex worry when Mary's date takes her out in a beat-up old car.

DR83.   **"Higher Learning"**   11/10/60
W: Hugh Wedlock & Howard Snyder   D: Jeffrey Hayden
GS: Richard Deacon (*Mr. Conroy*), Lester Maxwell (*Malcolm*)
Jeff takes an I.Q. test and is rated a genius, much to the surprise of the family. More confusion arises when he fails the entrance exam to a special school.

DR84.   **"Never Marry a Doctor"**   11/17/60
W: John Whedon   D: Andrew McCullough
GS: Eddie Firestone (*Les Dobson*), Maxine Stuart (*Ellen Cruikshank*), Pattee Chapman (*Kathie Dobson*)
No one wants to believe it is the down-on-his-luck handyman responsible for the missing twenty dollars.

DR85.   **"It Only Hurts When I Laugh"**   11/24/60
W: Douglas Morrow   D: Jeffrey Hayden
GS: Lindsay Workman (*Dr. Higgins*), Carter DeHaven Sr. (*Fred Miller*), Helen Kleeb (*Nurse Jane*), Fern Barry (*Nurse Ann*), Marjorie Owens (*Mrs. Adams*), Timmy Cletro (*Jimmy*)
Alex has his appendix removed and proves that doctors make the worst patients.

DR86.   **"The Model Daughter"**   12/1/60
W: Tom & Helen August   D: Robert Ellis Miller
GS: Annelle Hayes (*Taffy Cinders*), Henry Beckman (*Hal*)
Mary wants to be a fashion model, but Alex is skeptical about the modeling school she applies to.

DR87.   **"Decisions, Decisions, Decisions"**   12/8/60
W: Theodore & Mathilde Ferro   D: Jeffrey Hayden
GS: Jan Stine (*Roger*), Robert Santon (*Larry*), Andrew Colmar (*Young Man*), Harvey Korman (*Headwaiter*), Dick Wilson (*Waiter*), Adrienne Evans (*Girl*)
Mary makes her first adult decision when her dates for the evening run up the restaurant bill and can't pay for it.

DR88.   **"Donna Goes to a Reunion"**   12/15/60
W: John Whedon   D: Robert Ellis Miller
GS: Barbara Perry (*Buffie*), Fay Baker (*Hope*), Nesdon Booth (*Fred*)

When Donna learns that an old boyfriend will be at her class reunion, her nervousness arouses Alex's curiosity.

DR89. **"Someone Is Watching"**   12/22/60
W: John Whedon   D: Robert Ellis Miller
GS: Michael McGreevy (*Gordie*), Betsy Jones Moreland
(*Mrs. Pratt*), Stephen Pearson (*Eddie*)
Jeff feels responsible for a friend's bike accident, then learns the boy faked his injury to get attention.

DR90. **"Lean and Hungry Look"**   12/29/60
W: Tom & Helen August   D: Robert Ellis Miller
Alex criticizes Donna's willpower when she is on a diet. Then he finds he needs to lose weight himself.

DR91. **"Character Building"**   1/5/61
W: Clifford Goldsmith   D: Jeffrey Hayden
GS: Kristine Miller (*Edna*), Dani Nolan (*Mildred*), Pat Close (*Butch*)
Donna tries to instill responsibility in Mary and Jeff, and then gets caught behaving irresponsibly herself.

DR92. **"The World's Greatest Entertainer"**   1/12/61
W: Barbara Hammer   D: Norman Tokar
GS: Connie Sawyer (*Mrs. Lubner*)
In order to boost Jeff's ego, his family praises his impersonations. Then they must save him from embarrassment when he signs up for a talent show.

DR93. **"Variations on a Theme"**   1/19/61
W: John Whedon   D: Jeffrey Hayden
GS: Harvey Lembeck (*Al*), Reba Waters (*Ginny*), Paul Sullivan (*Fuzzy Cartwright*), Ludwig Stossel (*Piano Tuner*), John Indrisano (*Rudy*)
Mary conspires to outdo another girl at school by throwing a party and inviting a rock pianist.

DR94. **"The Stones Go to Hollywood"**   1/26/61
W: Phil Sharp   D: Ted Haworth
GS: George Sidney (*Himself*), Lassie (*Herself*), Midge Ware (*Secretary*), Phil Arnold (*Assistant Director*)
The Stones go to Hollywood, where director George Sidney gives them roles in his film "Pepe" (see F40).

DR95. **"Donna Directs a Play"**   2/2/61
W: Tom & Helen August   D: Robert Ellis Miller
GS: Jan Stine (*Johnny*), Eden Kessell (*Tracy*), Allen Emerson (*Gilbert Hardy*), David Macklin (*Doug*)
Donna takes over when the famous director leaves the community play Mary is starring in.

DR96. **"Trip to Nowhere"**   2/9/61
W: John Whedon   D: Robert Ellis Miller
GS: Ricky Klein (*Gordie*), Bill Baldwin (*Mr. Pratt*), Larry Hart (*Pete*)
Donna promises to take the kids camping while Alex is away.

DR97. "The Geisha Girl"   2/16/61
       W: Tom & Helen August   D: Norman Tokar
       GS: Miyoshi Umeki (*Mrs. Semple*), Douglas Dick (*Dr.
       Semple*), Arthur Hanson (*Ben*), Aline Towne (*Kay*),
       Rodney Bell (*Ed*), Sally Mansfield (*Beth*)
       Donna and Alex are outraged when their friends shun
       the new doctor's Oriental wife.

DR98. "The Busy People"   2/23/61
       W: Hugh Wedlock & Howard Snyder   D: James Neilson
       GS: Alix Talton (*Harriet*), Lindsay Workman (*Jim*),
       Fred Kruger (*Moresby*), Paul Barselow (*Fred*)
       Alex takes up painting when Donna and her friends
       decide their husbands need new interests.

DR99. "Tony Martin Visits"   3/2/61
       W: Hugh Wedlock & Howard Snyder, & Phil Sharp
       D: Robert Ellis Miller
       GS: Tony Martin (*Himself*), Herb Vigran (*Judge*), Roger
       Mobley (*Tony Jr.*), Owen Bush (*Cop*)
       Tony Martin meets Donna in traffic court, where they
       are both fighting tickets.

DR100. "Aunt Belle's Earnings"   3/9/61
       W: Henry Sharp   D: Robert Ellis Miller
       GS: Gladys Hurlbut (*Aunt Belle*), Will Wright (*Oliver*)
       Alex's aunt comes to town and is reunited with her
       old flame, a man whom Alex cannot stand.

DR101. "The Poodle Parlor"   3/16/61
       W: John Whedon   D: Jeffrey Hayden
       GS: Florence MacMichael (*Madeline*), Jack Albertson
       (*Jack*), Frank Wilcox (*George Heiser*)
       When their husbands claim that Donna and her friend
       have no business sense, they decide to open up a
       poodle parlor to prove them wrong.

DR102. "Mary's Heart Throb"   3/23/61
       W: John Whedon   D: Norman Tokar
       GS: Tommy Ivo (*Herbie*), Claude Johnson (*Rick Damon*),
       Wilton Graff (*Mr. Damon*), Sara Seegar (*Mrs. Damon*)
       While Mary is babysitting, the family's son returns
       home having dropped out of school.

DR103. "Donna's Helping Hand"   3/30/61
       W: John Whedon   D: Norman Tokar
       GS: Frances Robinson (*Myra*), Vladimir Sokoloff (*Dr.
       Steinhaus*), Robert Shayne (*Dr. Flanagan*), Stuart
       Nisbet (*Reporter*), Jeanne Tatum (*Woman*)
       Donna tries to get Alex to take the job as Board of
       Health Director.

DR104. "Merry Month of April"   4/6/61
       W: John Whedon   D: Robert Ellis Miller
       GS: Ruth Storey (*Nora*), Francis DeSales (*Harvey*),
       Lindsay Workman (*Dr. Jim Brady*), Hanna Landy
       (*Salesgirl*), Franklin Pinky Parker (*Judge*), Sheila
       Rogers (*Woman Waitress*)
       Donna has their income tax return prepared by a
       professional, but Alex wanted to do it himself.

DR105. **"Music Hath Charms"** 4/13/61
W: John Whedon D: Norman Tokar
GS: Lindsay Workman (*Dr. Jim Higgins*), Trudy Marshall
(*Mother*), Tony Haig (*Eddie*), Peter Oliphant (*Pete*),
Jimmy Gaines (*Jerry*)
Donna gives Alex a music box which plays "their song"
and Alex breaks it.

DR106. **"Let's Look at Love"** 4/20/61
W: Clifford Goldsmith D: Jeffrey Hayden
GS: Jan Stine (*Roger*), Robert Singer (*Stanley*), Ray
Baumann (*Jerry*)
Mary decides to give up dating when she sees two boys
flipping a coin to decide who is to take her out.

DR107. **"For Better or Worse"** 4/27/61
W: Phil Sharp & David R. Schwartz S: Nate Monaster
D: Norman Tokar
GS: Frances Robinson (*Myra*), Lindsay Workman (*Jim*),
Dort Clark (*Joe*), Reid Hammond (*Ed*)
Alex boasts that he doesn't need to ask his wife's
permission to go fishing like the others do. Donna
surprises him by saying no.

DR108. **"Jeff, the Treasurer"** 5/4/61
W: John Elliotte D: Jeffrey Hayden
GS: Doodles Weaver (*Mr. Perkins*), Karen Green (*Amy*),
Anne Loos (*Miss Haskell*), Kevin O'Neal (*First Boy*)
Jeff is entrusted with the class treasury, but
proceeds to lose the money.

DR109. **"The Good Guys and the Bad Guys"** 5/11/61
W: John Whedon D: Robert Ellis Miller
GS: Leonard Stone (*Mr. Trestle*), Vaughn Meadows
(*Jocko*), Stephen Talbot (*Lenny*), Bobby Clark
(*Gordie*), Michael Hart (*Eddie*), Miriam Tucker
(*Teacher*)
When Jeff is teased for joining the church choir, he
skips choir practice to train to fight the bullies.

DR110. **"Military School"** 5/18/61
W: Henry Sharp D: Robert Ellis Miller
GS: Chris Robinson (*Ken*), Tommy Ivo (*Herbie*),
Adrianne Ellis (*Claudette*)
Mary falls for her boyfriend's guest who is visiting
from military school.

DR111. **"Mary's Driving Lesson"** 5/25/61
W: Tom and Helen August D: Robert Ellis Miller
GS: Jimmy Hawkins (*Scotty*)
Mary asks her friend Scotty to teach her to drive and
their battles behind the wheel remind Donna of her
teenage driving lessons with Alex.

DR112. **"The Mustache"** 6/1/61
W: Phil Sharp D: Jeffrey Hayden
GS: Doodles Weaver (*Paul, the barber*)
Alex comes home from a hunting trip unshaven, and his
barber convinces him to keep the mustache. Donna
does all she can to convince him to get rid of it.

DR113. **"Mary's Little Lambs"**   6/8/61
W: Tom & Helen August   D: Jeffrey Hayden
GS: Doug Lambert (*Mark*), Karyn Kupcinet (*Jeannie*),
Peter   Oliphant   (*Johnnie*), Bobby Buntrock (*Crying
Child*)
Mary's pushy boyfriend gets her help setting up a
daycare center- in the Stone household.

DR114. **"One Starry Night"**   9/14/61
W: Sumner Long   D: Jeffrey Hayden
GS: James Darren, Johnny Darren
Mary has a date with a singer, but doesn't know who
he really is.

DR115. **"A Rose Is a Rose"**   9/21/61
GS: John Zaremba (*Mr. Smith*), Paul Engle (*Spike*)
Jeff does poorly on an English composition and unless
he   rewrites   it   he   can't   play   in   the father-son
football game with Alex.

DR116. **"The Close Shave"**   9/28/61
Jeff thinks he is growing a beard and asks permission
to buy a shaving kit.

DR117. **"The Mouse at Play"**   10/5/61
W: John Whedon   D: Jeffrey Hayden
GS: John Astin (*Eric, the hairdresser*), Cloris
Leachman (*Iris*)
While Alex is away at a convention, Donna decides to
change her hair and dyes it a much lighter shade.
Fearing that Alex won't approve of such a drastic
change, she has it dyed back before his return.

DR118. **"The Monster"**   10/12/61
A huge dog turns up at the Stones' and Jeff decides
to keep him. (See B93 for more information on "Coco"
the dog signed for the show.)

DR119. **"New Girl in Town"**   10/19/61
GS: Candy Moore
Donna tries to fix Jeff up with the new girl in town.

DR120. **"One of Those Days"**   10/26/61
Everything goes wrong for Alex and Donna as they try
to spend a day in the country.

DR121. **"All Is Forgiven"**   11/2/61
GS: William Windom
Alex and Donna reunite a fighting couple by trying to
get them to adopt a baby.

DR122. **"The Electrical Storm"**   11/9/61
GS: Richard Deacon
Jeff is expelled from school when he refuses to turn
in his friends.

DR123. **"The Paper Tycoon"**   11/16/61
Jeff takes over three paper routes and hires other
kids to work for him- keeping a healthy profit for
himself.

DR124. **"Private Tutor"** 11/23/61
The tutor Donna hires to help Mary with her French is
the same boy Mary secretly has a crush on.

DR125. **"Alex, the Professor"** 11/30/61
Alex gets unexpected results when he tries to use
psychology on his children.

DR126. **"The Fabulous O'Hara"** 12/7/61
GS: Cecil Kellaway
Jeff helps an orphan and his grandfather find a
permanent home.

DR127. **"Way of a Woman"** 12/14/61
When Mary's boyfriend breaks their skiing date, she
asks Alex to take her on his trip to Chicago.

DR128. **"A Very Bright Boy"** 12/21/61
GS: Johnny Crawford
The lazy but bright son of one of Donna's friends
comes for a visit.

DR129. **"The Toughest Kid in School"** 12/28/61
GS: Kirk Alyn
A new kid tries to impress Jeff by acting like a
delinquent.

DR130. **"Dr. Stone and His Horseless Carriage"** 1/11/62
GS: Oliver McGowan, Gale Gordon
A patient gives Alex a 1911 horseless buggy for
payment of his services.

DR131. **"For Angie with Love"** 1/18/62
GS: Candy Moore (Angie)
Jeff tries to impress his girlfriend Angie with
expensive gifts.

DR132. **"Aloha, Kimi"** 1/25/62
GS: Miyoshi Umeki (Kimi)
Alex goes to Hawaii to help a girl who was hurt in a
surfboard accident.

DR133. **"Donna's Primadonna"** 2/1/62
GS: James Stacy
Mary's decision to skip college and become a singer
doesn't sit well with Donna.

DR134. **"Explorers Ten"** 2/8/62
Jeff's club tries to earn enough money to buy a
telescope.

DR135. **"The New Office"** 2/15/62
GS: Alan Hewitt
Alex decides to move his office from the house to a
new medical center.

DR136. **"The Golden Trap"** 2/22/62
Donna and Alex go away, leaving Jeff and the house in
Mary's care.

DR137. **"Free Flight"**   3/1/62
GS: William Lanteau
Donna gets a free flight after writing a letter of
complaint to the head of an airline.

DR138. **"Wide Open Spaces"**   3/8/62
GS: William Windom
When Donna and Alex visit their friend's farm, they
find the couple unhappy and longing for city life.

DR139. **"The Fire Ball"**   3/15/62
GS: Candy Moore (*Angie*)
Jeff and Angie get the leads in the school play.

DR140. **"Once Upon a Timepiece"**   3/22/62
Donna buys Alex a watch in a pawn shop and then tries
to help the former owner.

DR141. **"Hilldale 500"**   3/29/62
GS: Candy Moore (*Angie*)
Alex helps Jeff build a race cart to enter in a race.

DR142. **"Winner Take All"**   4/5/62
GS: Ken Lynch, Allan Hunt
Alex tries to help a father who is disappointed in
his son's pitching at a baseball game.

DR143. **"Skin Deep"**   4/12/62
Mary learns a lesson in beauty when she turns down a
date with a boy who has big ears.

DR144. **"The Fortune Teller"**   4/19/62
Donna plays fortune teller at a bazaar, and her
bizarre predictions start coming true!

DR145. **"Man of Action"**   4/26/62
Alex plays babysitter when everyone else is too busy.

DR146. **"Donna Meets Roberta"**   5/3/62
GS: Roberta Sherwood, Gale Gordon, Robert Lansing
Alex buys a house when he learns that the property
values are about to increase.

DR147. **"The Caravan"**   5/10/62
GS: Al Checco
Donna wants the family to spend their summer vacation
on the road in a rented caravan.

DR148. **"The Swingin' Set"**   5/17/62
Jeff tries to get a prom date for his buddy.

DR149. **"On to Fairview"**   5/24/62
GS: Paul Tripp
Jeff tries to earn enough money to buy Donna a
crystal pendant.

DR150. **"The Man in the Mask"**   5/31/62
GS: Don Drysdale (*Himself*)
Jeff is chosen to umpire a girl's baseball game and
he gets some coaching from Don Drysdale.

DR151. **"The Father Image"** 6/7/62
Alex tries to solve his family's problems along with those of one of his patients.

DR152. **"Dear Wife"** 6/14/62
Alex and Donna think Mary is planning to elope.

DR153. **"Mister Nice Guy"** 9/20/62
W: Paul West   D: Jeffrey Hayden
GS: Alan Carney
Mary is suspicious of Jeff's motives when he suddenly becomes kind and considerate towards her before her departure for college.

DR154. **"Mrs. Stone and Dr. Hyde"** 9/27/62
W: Barbara Hammer   D: Gene Nelson
GS: Marge Redmond (*Alma*), Renee Godfrey (*Gloria*), Sally Mansfield (*Alice*), Annelle Hayes (*Mrs. Bolton*), Bobby Horan (*Jimmy*), Frances Rey (*Mrs. Calder*), Dick Wilson (*Mr. Drucker*)
Donna fills in for Alex's vacationing nurse, and she finds him to be a tyrant to work for.

DR155. **"To Be a Boy"** 10/4/62
W: Paul West   D: Gene Nelson
GS: Brooke Bundy (*Joanne*), Darryl Richard (*Smitty*), Carol Sydes (*Caroline*)
Jeff and Smitty make a vow to stop dating in order to save enough money to build a boat. Mary's pretty young friend Joanne provides a complication when Jeff finds her hiding under his bed.

DR156. **"Who Needs Glasses?"** 10/11/62
W: Sumner Long   D: Jeffrey Hayden
GS: Harvey Korman (*Dr. Alison, the optometrist*), Darryl Richard (*Smitty*), Candy Moore (*Angie*)
Jeff tries to prove that he needs glasses, because he thinks they'll make him look older.

DR157. **"Mary, Mary, Quite Contrary"** 10/18/62
GS: Cheryl Holdridge (*Pat Walker*)
Mary decides it's time to leave home and moves into the college dormitory.

DR158. **"My Dad"** 10/25/62
W: Barbara Hammer Avedon   D: Gene Nelson
GS: Darryl Richard (*Smitty*), Ray Montgomery (*Mr. Smith*), Dick Foster (*Boy*), Ken Strange (*Policeman*)
Housecalls and emergencies keep Alex from spending time with the family, and Jeff feels neglected. After Alex misses Jeff's show at school, Jeff sings his song "My Dad" for the family.

DR159. **"Fine Feathers"** 11/1/62
W: Andy White   D: Gene Nelson
GS: Darryl Richard (*Smitty*), Tom Gilleran (*Herb*), Donnie Baker (*Boy*), Bee Peters (*Mrs. Bentley*)
Jeff takes in a lost bird, but doesn't want to take responsibility for it until he learns that it may be valuable.

DR160. "Rebel with a Cause"   11/8/62
       W: Barbara Hammer Avedon   D: Gene Nelson
       GS: Harvey Korman (*Carver Melville*), Harold Gould
       (*Cal Winslow*), William Zuckert (*Jason Farnum*), Dick
       Wilson (*Mr. Carothers*), Helena Carroll (*Jeanette*)
       Donna is asked to participtate in a survey on the
       "average woman," and is angered at just how average
       everyone thinks she is.

DR161. "Big Star"   11/15/62
       W: Barbara Hammer Avedon & Paul West
       D: Jeffrey Hayden
       GS: Jerry Lanning (*Clay Shannon*), Arthur Malet
       (*Professor Raskin*), Betsy Jones Moreland (*Geri*)
       Mary discovers a great singing talent in a shy
       gardener's assistant, but the boy has no confidence.
       Shelly Fabares sings "Big Star."

DR162. "Man to Man"   11/22/62
       W: Paul West   D: Andrew McCullough
       GS: Darryl Richard (*Smitty*), Tony Owen, Jr. (*Rick*),
       Harry Korshak (*Jerry*), Nancy Spry (*Cheryl*), Patricia
       Lyon (*Joe*), Connie Holiday (*Jeannie*), Susan White
       (*Lorraine*)
       Alex and Jeff go camping so that they can spend some
       time together.   But the trip turns out to be a plot
       cooked up by Jeff to meet his friends.   Donna's son
       Tony Jr. appears as one of Jeff's friends.

DR163. "The Baby Buggy"   11/29/62
       W: John Whedon   D: Andrew McCullough
       GS: Fay Bainter (*Doctor Harriet Robey*), Hayden Rorke
       (*Joe McVey*), Richard Deacon (*Mr. Moorehead*), Jerry
       Trump (*Delivery Boy*), George Dockstader (*Policeman*)
       Everyone chips in to buy the elderly baby doctor a
       new car to replace her old clunker.

DR164. "The Make-Over Man"   12/6/62
       W: Ralph Goodman   D: Gene Nelson
       GS: Jim Stacy (*Steve Callahan*), Bob Rodgers (*Coach*),
       Shary Marshall (*Gloria*), Bea Shaw (*Woman*), Allan Hunt
       Mary tries to change her boyfriend into the kind of
       man she wants him to be, but succeeds only in making
       him unhappy.

DR165. "The Winning Ticket"   12/13/62
       W: Phil Davis   D: Andrew McCullough
       GS: Darryl Richard (*Smitty*), Jeff De Benning (*Mr.
       Werner*), William Visteen (*Mr. Anderson*), Edmund
       Williams (*Insurance Man*), Carolyn Morin (*Woman*), Anja
       Comer (*Barbie*), Thomas A. Gleason (*Announcer*)
       Jeff wins a new car with a raffle ticket he found,
       and then has to return it to it's rightful owner.

DR166. "The Soft Touch"   12/20/62
       W: Ben Gershman & Milton Pascal D: Andrew McCullough
       When Alex tries to collect his patients' overdue
       bills and Jeff tries to collect money his friends owe
       him, Donna and Mary discover that the men in the
       family are softies.

DR167. **"Jeff Stands Alone"** 12/27/62
W: Barbara Hammer Avedon   D: Andrew McCullough
GS: Darryl Richard (*Smitty*), Jim Stacy (*Sandy*),
Leslie Wales (*April Poston*), William Lanteau (*Mr.
Jepson*), Ted Bergen (*Tony*), A.G. Vitanza (*Hotel
Clerk*)
Jeff spends a weekend in a strange town with no
money, just to prove that he can make it on his own.

DR168. **"Just a Little Wedding"** 1/3/63
W: Barbara Hammer Avedon   D: Barry Shear
GS: Binnie Barnes (*Binnie Haversham*), Brenda Scott,
(*Marcia Haversham*), Robert Hogan (*Bob Parker*), Carl
Milletaire (*Marcel*), Carolyn Morin (*Woman at Airport*)
Donna agrees to let Mary's friends get married at
their house, but has second thoughts when the girl's
domineering mother arrives and takes over.

DR169. **"A Woman's Place"** 1/10/63
GS: Joyce Aehle (*Margaret*), Rodney Bell, Edmund
Williams, Evan Thompson (*Reporters*)
When Donna spends all her time campaigning for town
council, the house falls apart and Alex dreams he's
the First Lady.

DR170. **"The Chinese Horse"** 1/17/63
W: Paul West   D: Gene Nelson
GS: Karen Kadler (*Gloria*), Stephen Roberts (*Burt
Rafferty*), Jerry Douglas (*Officer Larson*), Joseph
Downing (*Man*), Connie Madison (*Girl at Auction*), Paul
Winchell (*Auctioneer*)
Donna buys a Chinese horse at an auction for a
strange woman in dark glasses. Spawned by Jeff's
imagination and some strange happenings that night,
the family gets caught up in mystery and suspense.

DR171. **"The New Look"** 1/24/63
W: Phil Davis   D: Andrew McCullough
GS: Yale Summers (*Howard*), Duke Howard (*Bob*), Karla
Most (*Dorine*), Allan Hunt (*Bill*)
Mary resents her "wholesome" reputation and wants to
be more flamboyant.

DR172. **"A Way of Her Own"** 1/31/63
W: Paul West   D: Andrew McCullough
GS: Patty Petersen (*Trisha*), Charles Carlson (*Fred
Hawley*)
Eight year old Trisha follows the Stones home from
the park and decides to stay. When they discover
that the little girl is an orphan, the family
"adopts" her. Trisha is played by Paul Petersen's
real life sister, Patty.

DR173. **"Three Is a Family"** 2/7/63
W: Paul West   D: Andrew McCullough
GS: Patty Petersen (*Trisha*), Jimmy Hawkins (*Scotty*)
Mary feels jealous of the attention Trisha is
receiving from the family. When the two girls are
left alone for the evening, they work things out.

DR174. **"Big Sixteen"**   2/14/63
W: Barbara Hammer Avedon   D: Gene Nelson
GS: Brooke Bundy (*Joanne*), Darryl Richard (*Smitty*),
Carol Weaver (*Jeanette*)
When Jeff and Joanne have a fight just before his
sixteenth birthday, Jeff goes after an older woman.

DR175. **"Pioneer Woman"**   2/21/63
W: Barbara Hammer Avedon   D: Gene Nelson
GS: Jim Davis (*Red*), Hal K. Dawson (*Mountaineer*),
Tony Owen, Jr. (*Roger Griffin*), Judi Hersey (*Wendy
Simms*), Diana Bradshaw (*Granddaughter*)
Donna and Mary follow the men up to a cabin mountains
to prove that they are not soft and pampered.

DR176. **"The House on the Hill"**   2/28/63
W: Barney Slater & Michael Cramoy   D: Gene Nelson
GS: Kathryn Givney (*Mrs. Allison*), Joseph Downing
(*Eric*),   Olive   Dunbar   (*Pauline*), Angela Greene
(*Grace*), Dorothy Lovett   (*Edie*),   Patty Petersen
(*Trisha*), Thomas Anthony (*Police Sergeant*)
Donna visits the home of an old recluse and finds
herself trapped there against her will.

DR177. **"Where the Stones Are"**   3/7/63
W: Seymour Friedman   D: Gene Nelson
GS: Mikki Jamison (*Bonnie*), Patty Petersen (*Trisha*),
Darla Banks (*Darla Banks*), Irina Alexander (*Judy*)
The Stones follow Mary on a weekend trip with her
friends in order to check up on her.

DR178. **"The Two Doctor Stones"**   3/14/63
W: Barbara Hammer Avedon   D: Barry Shear
GS: Bob Crane (*Dr. Dave Blevins*), Patty Petersen
(*Trisha*)
Alex and Donna try to go away for the weekend, but
Trisha changes their plans by getting sick.

DR179. **"Everywhere That Mary Goes"**   3/21/63
W: Paul West   D: Gene Nelson
GS: Steve Clinton (*Clovis Bohmer*), Ida Mae McKenzie
(*Lottie Bohmer*), Hal Barringer (*Orville Bohmer*),
Jimmy Baird (*Emory Peck*), Valora Noland (*Vinnie
Sayres*), Skip Torgerson (*Glenn*), Buddy Hart (*Robbie*)
A new boy at Mary's school follows her everywhere to
protect her from other boys.

DR180. **"The Handy Man"**   3/28/63
W: Paul West   D: Andrew McCullough
GS: Doodles   Weaver   (*Charlie Brubaker*), Jeff De
Benning (*Mr. Fletcher*), Patty Petersen (*Trisha*),
Eloise Hardt (*Gloria Simms*)
Donna is the only person who sees the solution to the
problems of a handyman who can't fix anything and an
ice cream man who hates kids.

DR181. **"Friends and Neighbors"**   4/4/63
W: Barbara Hammer Avedon   D: Barry Shear
GS: Bob Crane (*Dr. Dave Kelsey*), Ann McCrea (*Midge
Kelsey*), Patty Petersen (*Trisha*)

Alex's friend and his new bride buy the house next door to the Stones. Donna tries to transform the wife into a good housekeeper.

DR182. **"Boys and Girls"** 4/11/63
GS: Jimmy Hawkins (*Scotty*), Mimsy Farmer (*Joanne Wells*), Cheryl Miller (*Becky*), Glenn Perry (*Ted*)
Jeff and Mary attend a college dance, and their dates run off together.

DR183. **"All Those Dreams"** 4/18/63
W: Barbara Hammer Avedon   D: Gene Nelson
GS: Don Drysdale, Ginger Drysdale, Kelly Drysdale (*Themselves*), Paul Winchell (*Mr. Morton*), Patty Petersen (*Trisha*), Suzanne Price (*Rosemary*)
The Stone family travels to Chicago, where Jeff tries to get in touch with Don Drysdale. Jeff feels hurt when he thinks his old pal is brushing him off.

DR184. **"All Women Are Dangerous"** 4/25/63
GS: Lori Martin (*Joyce*), Janet Landgard (*Sabrina*), Darryl Richard (*Smitty*), Sherry Granato (*Gwen*)
Two girls are battling for an invitation to a party from Jeff, but he can't make up his mind.

DR185. **"The Big Wheel"** 5/2/63
W: Barbara Hammer Avedon   D: Barry Shear
GS: Patty Petersen (*Trisha*), Yale Summers (*Howard*), Buddy Lewis (*Manny*), Glenn Perry (*Bill*), Scott Elliott (*Man on Bus*), Joyce Morrill (*Joyce*)
Jeff buys an old bus at an auction, but finds it's more trouble than it's worth.

DR186. **"Day of the Hero"** 5/9/63
GS: Darryl Richard (*Smitty*), Sherry Granato (*Rosemary*), Mary Jane Saunders (*Dolores*), Jil Jarmyn (*Teacher*)
Jeff asks a girl to the prom, but when he thinks he's going to be voted class president, he invites a different girl.

Beginning with the 1963-64 season, Patty Petersen (*Trisha*), Bob Crane (*Dr. Dave Kelsey*) and Ann McCrea (*Midge Kelsey*) became regular cast members.

DR187. **"Brighten the Corner"** 9/26/63
GS: Oliver McGowan
Trisha messes up the house just as guests arrive.

DR188. **"Whatever You Wish"** 10/3/63
GS: Whit Bissell, Dort Clark
Jeff saves the life of a rich woman's daughter, and she offers him anything he wants in return.

DR189. **"House Divided"** 10/10/63
The Stones and the Kelseys share a summer cabin.

DR190. **"The Boys in 309"** 10/17/63
Jeff is hurt during a football game.

DR191. **"The Bigger They Are"**   10/24/63
GS: Jacques Aubuchon, Peter Leeds
A freeway will be built on Donna's land, unless she
can convince a farmer to allow them to build on his
land.

DR192. **"It Grows on Trees"**   10/31/63
GS: Henry Kulky, Darryl Richard (*Smitty*)
Jeff and Smitty try to earn money for a skiing trip
by selling trees.

DR193. **"Mary Comes Home"**   11/7/63
Donna plans a surprise party for Mary's visit home.

DR194. **"Post Time"**   11/14/63
GS: George Chandler
Jeff and his friends borrow a race horse in a scheme
to raise money for band uniforms.

DR195. **"Sweet Mystery of Wife"**   11/21/63
Alex gets a telegram and forgets to read it, sparking
Donna's curiosity.

DR196. **"What Are Friends For?"**   11/28/63
W: Barbara Avedon   D: Barry Shear
GS: Darryl Richard (*Smitty*), Diane Bradshaw
(*Caroline*), Terry Reno (*Amy Carter*), Owen Pavitt (*Dr.
Carter*)
Jeff gets Smitty to take his place on a date Alex set
up for him.

DR197. **"A Touch of Glamour"**   12/5/63
GS: Alice Pearce
Donna returns a gown Alex bought for her because she
thinks it is too expensive.

DR198. **"Air Date"**   12/12/63
Jeff makes a date with a girl he "met" on a CB radio.

DR199. **"Moon-Shot"**   12/19/63
GS: John Banner, Darryl Richard (*Smitty*)
Jeff and Smitty sell tickets to a dance.

DR200. **"Nice Work"**   12/26/63
Jeff gets a job escorting a girl around town.

DR201. **"First Addition"**   1/2/64
GS: Sam Jaffe, Walter Janowitz, Mary Wickes
Donna remembers what her life was like when Mary was
born.

DR202. **"The Combo"**   1/9/64
Jeff tries to get his musical group a gig at a girl's
club.

DR203. **"Who's Rockin' the Partnership?"**   1/16/64
GS: Darryl Richard (*Smitty*)
Jeff and Smitty operate a gas station while the owner
is away for the summer.

DR204. "Something Funny Happened on the Way to the Altar"
Dave tells the Stones the story of how he met Midge
on a blind date.   1/23/64

DR205. "Today I Am a Girl"   1/30/64
Donna tries to transform tomboy Trisha into a lady.

DR206. "Will the Real Chicken Please Stand Up?"   2/6/64
GS: William Lanteau
Donna teaches Midge to drive a car.

DR207. "Guest in the Nursery"   2/13/64
Dave Kelsey finds a baby fawn, and Trisha wants to
keep it.

DR208. "Home Sweet Homemaker"   2/20/64
Dave and Midge fight over her cooking, and Dave takes
shelter at the Stones.

DR209. "Teamwork"   2/27/64
GS: Peter Robbins
Trisha and her friends help Donna around the house.

DR210. "Neither a Borrower Nor a Lender Be"   3/5/64
Donna tries to get Midge to repay all of the money
she lent her.

DR211. "Pandemonium in the Condominium"   3/12/64
GS: Fritz Feld
The Stones and the Kelseys economize by buying one
washer and one set of golf clubs and sharing both.

DR212. "Day for Remembering"   3/19/64
Jeff's graduation is the setting for an episode of
flashbacks from previous shows.

DR213. "One Little Word"   3/26/64
Donna tries to discover the meaning of the word Alex
keeps saying in his sleep.

DR214. "Love Letters Are for Burning"   4/2/64
GS: Kathleen Crowley
Dave is worried that an old girlfriend will use his
love letters to her as subject matter for her next
book.

DR215. "Four's a Crowd"   4/19/64
The Stones and the Kelseys feel they are spending too
much time together.

DR216. "My Son the Catcher"   4/16/64
GS: Don Drysdale, Leo Durocher, Willie Mays, William
Bramley
Jeff decides that baseball is more important than
going to school.

DR217. "The Pros and the Cons"   4/23/64
Donna and Midge try to learn how to play golf in
order to teach their husbands a lesson.

DR218. **"Operation Anniversary"**   9/17/64
D: Fred DeCordova
Jeff tries to earn some money to take Donna and Alex
out to dinner for their anniversary.

DR219. **"Dad Drops By"**   9/24/64
Alex's father comes for a visit and stirs up trouble.

DR220. **"Play Ball"**   10/1/64
GS: Leo   Durocher,   Don   Drysdale,   Willie   Mays
(*Themselves*)
Three   baseball   stars   join   the   hospital   staff's
charity baseball game.

DR221. **"Who's Who on 202?"**   10/8/64
GS: Richard Conte, Byron Morrow
Donna thinks the man   who   helped   her   when   her car
broke down is an escaped convict.

DR222. **"The Daughter Complex"**   10/15/64
Mary   is   studying   psychology,   and begins analyzing
everyone in her family.

DR223. **"The Tycoons"**   10/22/64
Alex and Dave invest in the stock market   and plan to
buy color TV sets with their profits.

DR224. **"Instant Family"**   10/29/64
Donna and   Alex go out of town, leaving the kids with
Dave and Midge.

DR225. **"Royal Flush"**   11/5/64
GS: Vito Scotti, Maxie Rosenbloom
Two con men pose as visiting royalty.

DR226. **"Circumstantial Evidence"**   11/12/64
Alex finds a picture of Donna's old boyfriend   in the
house and becomes jealous.

DR227. **"Anyone Can Drive"**   11/19/64
GS: Janet Landgard (*Karen*)
Jeff tries to teach his girlfriend how to drive.

DR228. **"Surprise Surprise"**   11/26/64
Alex   and   Dave   plan   a   surprise birthday party for
Midge.

DR229. **"Quads of Trouble"**   12/3/64
GS: Dr. Edward R. Annis
A pregnant woman can't make   it   to   the   hospital in
time, and Alex delivers her quadruplets in his house.
Now the house has become a nursery.

DR230. **"Donna's Bank Account"**   12/10/64
Donna   tries   to   retrieve   a   bad   check   before   it
bounces.

DR231. **"It's All in the Cards"**   12/17/64
Midge takes   up fortune   telling and believes she has
mystic powers.

DR232. **"Old Faithful"**   12/24/64
       GS: Jimmy Hawkins (*Scotty*)
       Mary learns that Scotty has been dating another girl.

DR233. **"Overture in A-Flat"**   12/31/64
       GS: Darryl Richard (*Smitty*)
       Jeff and Smitty get their own apartment, but can't
       get rid of their freeloading friends.

DR234. **"Thy Name Is Woman"**   1/7/65
       A strange man takes an interest in Donna, and Midge
       becomes jealous of the attention.

DR235. **"Joe College"**   1/14/65
       Alex's father retires and enrolls at Jeff's college.

DR236. **"Painter Go Home"**   1/21/65
       GS: John Fielder, Nora Marlowe
       The man Donna hired to paint the livingroom makes
       himself at home.

DR237. **"Home Wreckonomics"**   1/28/65
       GS: Janet Landgard (*Karen*)
       Karen must run the finances of a home for her Home Ec
       class, and Midge offers her home for the experiment.

DR238. **"The Windfall"**   2/4/65
       GS: Oliver McGowan
       Jeff buys a suitcase at an auction and finds over
       five hundred dollars inside.

DR239. **"Now You See It Now You Don't"**   2/11/65
       GS: Buster Keaton
       Donna tries to get the car fixed before Alex notices
       the dent caused by the truck that hit her.

DR240. **"The Gift Shop"**   2/18/65
       GS: Ellen Corby, Peter Hobbs
       Jeff is bored with his job in a slow gift shop.

DR241. **"The Stamp Collector"**   2/25/65
       GS: John Hiestand
       Donna and Alex go to cash in their trading stamps and
       can't agree on what to purchase with them.

DR242. **"Peacocks on the Roof"**   3/4/65
       Alex is the only person who keeps seeing animals in
       their yard. Is he seeing things?

DR243. **"Guests, Guests, Who Needs Guests?"**   3/11/65
       Dave's goddaughter is visiting from college, and
       Donna invites her to dinner.

DR244. **"The Unheroic Hero"**   3/18/65
       GS: Frank Gerstle, Allan Hunt
       Jeff's friend saves a dog that ran into a mine.

DR245. **"That Mysterious Smile"**   3/25/65
       GS: Barry Atwater, Michael Fox, Kim Darby, Cheryl
       Miller, Robert Fortier

Jeff writes a note to a girl inviting her on a skiing trip, but the note is given to the wrong girl and Jeff doesn't know how to break the date.

DR246. "The Rolling Stones"   4/1/65
GS: Aron Kincaid
The Stones and the Kelseys plan to spend a weekend together on a boat.

DR247. "Indoor Outing"   4/8/65
GS: Jim Davis, Al Checco, James Stacy
Donna stays home with Trisha when she gets sick and they can't go on their planned fishing trip. Donna tells Trisha about past fishing and camping trips.

Bob Crane left the regular cast at the end of the 1964-65 season to star in "Hogan's Heroes."

DR248. "Pop Goes Theresa!"   9/16/65
W: Paul West   D: Andrew McCullough
GS: Warren Stevens (*Mr. Brad Marshall*), Tisha Sterling (*Theresa Marshall*), Milton Frome (*Desk Sergeant*), Jimmy Hawkins (*Scotty*), Janet Landgard (*Karen*), Darryl Richard (*Smitty*), Frank Corsaro (*Murphy*), Karl Lukas (*Police Officer*), Gary Waynesmith (*Blake*), Dan Dalton (*Guitarist*)
Jeff's date, a girl raised by an overly strict father, suddenly goes wild and gets herself and Jeff arrested.

DR249. "With This Ring"   9/23/65
W: Don Richman & Janet Carlson   D: Lawrence Dobkin
GS: Ann McCrea (*Midge*), Janet Landgard (*Karen*), Jonathan Hole (*Mr. Martindale*), Jean Vanderpyl (*Mom Stone*), Jamie Farr (*The Waiter*), Kim Higgins (*Cynthia Collins*), Carl Betz (*Samuel J. Stone*)
Donna loses her wedding ring, but is afraid to tell Alex so she buys a cheap lookalike.

DR250. "The Boy Meets Girl Machine"   9/30/65
W: Paul West   D: E.W. Swackhamer
GS: Candy Moore (*Bernice*), Robert Ellenstein (*Dean Whittaker*), Jimmy Hawkins (*Scotty*), Darryl Richard (*Smitty*), Gary Waynesmith (*Willie*), Marianne Ittleson (*Secretary*), Jimmy Baird (*Joel*), Murray MacLeod (*Boy*)
Jeff and Scotty use a computer named Herman to pair up boys and girls for a Get Acquainted Party.

DR251. "Think Mink"   10/7/65
W: David Braverman & Bob Marcus   D: Lawrence Dobkin
GS: Ann McCrea (*Midge*), Virginia Vincent (*Mrs. Bellflower*), Molly Dodd (*Mrs. Randall*), Dick Wilson (*Mr. Hodges*), Peg Shirley (*Millie*), Kirk Alyn (*Man*)
Donna and Midge aren't sure which of them won a mink coat since they shared the cost of the raffle ticket.

DR252. "Four on the Floor"   10/14/65
W: Paul West   D: E.W. Swackhamer
GS: Janet Landgard (*Karen*), Jimmy Hawkins (*Scotty*), Laurence Haddon (*Mr. Henshaw*)

Karen's uncle sells Jeff a car, but the car soon stops running.

DR253. **"Charge!"** 10/21/65
W: Sam Locke & Joel Rapp   D: Jerrold Bernstein
GS: Arch Johnson (*Mr. Nelson*), Ann McCrea (*Midge*), Helen Clark (*Miss Rogers*), Dayna Ceder (*Miss Carson*)
A department store rejects Donna's credit application, but opens a charge account for Trisha's pet monkey.

DR254. **"Do Me a Favor- Don't Do Me Any Favors"** 10/28/65
W: Joel Rapp & Sam Locke   D: Lawrence Dobkin
GS: Lloyd Corrigan (*Professor James Caldwell*), Janet Landgard (*Karen*), Jimmy Hawkins (*Scotty*), Mary Treen (*Mrs. Larson*), Stephen Roberts (*Dean Shelby*)
Jeff fights to save Professor Caldwell from being forced into retirement. After Donna and Alex join in the fight, they learn the professor wants to retire.

DR255. **"Trees"** 11/4/65
W: Nathaniel Curtis   D: Andrew McCullough
GS: Ann McCrea (*Midge*), Paul Reed (*Commissioner Trimmit*), Maxine Stuart (*Helena Whitcomb*), Karl Lukas (*Mr. Swanson*), Pauline Myers (*Ethel Featherspoon*), Anne Bellamy (*Louise*), Aline Towne (*Helen*), Penny Kunard (*Julie*)
Donna fights against uniformity when the town wants to uproot the carob tree in front of her house and plant an elm tree like all the others on the street.

DR256. **"Author! Author!"** 11/11/65
W: Barbara Avedon   D: Jerrold Bernstein
GS: Ann McCrea (*Midge*)
Donna secretly tries her hand at writing and chooses her family as her topic.

DR257. **"The Big League Shock"** 11/18/65
GS: Mark Slade, Charles Lane, Dennis Cross
A student forges Alex's name on a prescription for pep pills.

DR258. **"The Gladiators"** 11/25/65
GS: Lee Patrick
Alex's father and Midge's mother fall for each other while both are visiting Hilldale. Carl Betz plays Dr. Stone and his father.

DR259. **"Rallye Round the Girls, Boys"** 12/2/65
GS: Dabney Coleman, Candy Moore, Sandy Descher, Jimmy Hawkins, Arthur Adams
Jeff believes that women wouldn't understand a car rally and then finds himself racing against two who are out to prove him wrong.

DR260. **"Slipped Disc"** 12/9/65
GS: Janis Hansen
A critic at a college party tells Jeff and his band that they should record their songs, and soon the boys are trying to raise the money to cut a record.

DR261. "Uncle Jeff Needs You"   12/16/65
        W: Sam Locke & Joel Rapp   D: Lawrence Dobkin
        GS: DeForest Kelley (*Mr. Williams*), Janet Landgard
        (*Karen*), June Whitley Taylor (*Mrs. Williams*), Enid
        Jaynes (*Miss Carson*), Kevin Tate (*Lennie*), Dean Moray
        (*Billy Williams*), Billy Corcoran (*Gregg Williams*),
        Edward Rosson (*Spike*)
        Jeff tries to recruit two boys for summer camp so
        that he can get a job as a counselor.

DR262. "Never Look a Gift Horse in the Mouth"   12/23/65
        GS: Betsy Jones Moreland, Gary Waynesmith
        When the Stones agree to take care of a friend's
        cottage on Echo Lake, Jeff sees it as the perfect
        place to throw a fraternity party.

DR263. "How to Handle Women"   12/30/65
        W: Andrew McCullough   D: Andrew McCullough
        GS: Linda Gaye Scott (*Deborah*), Candy Moore (*Bebe*),
        Jimmy Hawkins (*Scotty*), Darryl Richard (*Smitty*),
        Chanin Hale (*Myrtle*), Cathy Ferrar (*Susan*)
        Jeff and his friends try to prove that men are the
        stronger sex by dominating their girlfriends.

DR264. "My Son, the Councilman"   1/6/66
        GS: Paul Reed, Buddy Lewis, John Qualen
        Jeff runs for councilman after the Commissioner
        threatens to close the city park.

DR265. "Do It Yourself Donna"   1/15/66
        W: Lou Shaw   D: Lee Philips
        GS: Sandy Kenyon (*Salesman*), Bonnie Beecher (*Julie*),
        Ann McCrea (*Midge Kelsey*), Darryl Richard (*Smitty*)
        Donna and Alex spend weeks attempting to assemble a
        complicated stereo set for Jeff's birthday. When
        Jeff sees what a mess they've made, he and Smitty
        sneak in behind them each night to fix it.

DR266. "When I Was Your Age"   1/22/66
        W: Jack Raymond   D: Andrew McCullough
        GS: Candy Moore (*Bebe Barnes*), John Stephenson (*Ben
        Barnes*), Hollis Irving (*Harriet Barnes*), Charles
        Alvin Bell (*Clerk*)
        Donna and Alex try frantically to stop Jeff and Bebe
        from getting married.

DR267. "Calling Willie Mays"   1/29/66
        W: Jack Harvey & Irving Taylor   D: Lawrence Dobkin
        GS: Willie Mays (*Himself*), Edmon Ryan (*Dr. Grayson*),
        Amzie Strickland (*Mrs. Grayson*), Jordan Whitfield
        (*1st Ticket Clerk*), Baynes Barron (*2nd Ticket Clerk*),
        Jimmy Cross (*Scalper*), Nancy Spry (*Vickie*)
        Willie Mays reserves two seats at a Giants game for
        his friends the Stones, but Donna, Alex and Jeff each
        show up with a guest.

DR268. "All This and Voltaire Too?"   2/5/66
        W: Erna Lazarus   D: Lawrence Dobkin
        GS: Barbara Shelley (*Paulette*), Ann McCrea (*Midge*),
        Stanley Adams (*Voltaire*), Naomi Stevens (*Madame

Voltaire),   Paul   Steyer   (*Malcolm*),   Lynn   Carey
(*Jeannine*)
Donna   and   Midge   take   French   lessons   from   Monsieur
Voltaire, the owner of a French restaurant.

DR269. **"The Return of Mark"**   2/12/66
W: Barbara Avedon & Ray Singer   S: Barbara Avedon
D: Lee Philips
GS: Warren Stevens (*Mark Claridge*), Ann McCrea
(*Midge*), June Chandler (*Airline Girl*)
Donna's old boyfriend, now a millionaire, comes for a
visit and Alex can't hide his jealousy.

DR270. **"Is There a Small Hotel?"**   2/19/66
W: Laurence Marks & Ronny Pearlman
S: Laurence Marks   D: Andrew McCullough
GS: Ann McCrea (*Midge*), Peter Leeds (*Postman*), Arte
Johnson (*Crandall*), Nora Marlowe (*Mrs. Barton*),
Judson Pratt (*Metcalfe*), William Lanteau (*Mr.
Phillips*), James Hong (*Jim*)
The Stones decide to vacation in California, but
everyone thinks they should go someplace else.

DR271. **"No More Parties- Almost"**   2/26/66
W: Clifford Goldsmith   D: Andrew McCullough
GS: Ann McCrea (*Midge*), Gene Blakely (*Mr. Kingsley*),
Alice Backes (*Mrs. McCracken*), Anne Bellamy (*Mrs.
Kingsley*), Penny Kunard (*Isobel*), Kirk Alyn (*Steve
Slocum*), Jeff Burton (*Mailman*)
Donna and Alex, exhausted after weeks of social
engagements, want to get out of a friend's dinner
party. Then they learn that they weren't invited.

DR272. **"So You Really Think You're Young at Heart"**   3/5/66
W: Rick Mittleman   D: Andrew McCullough
GS: Ann McCrea (*Midge*), Paul Bryar (*Huckster*), Bobby
Johnson (*Attendant*)
Donna and Midge set out to prove that Alex and Dave
aren't getting old.

DR273. **"What Price Home?"**   3/12/66
W: Andrew McCullough   D: Andrew McCullough
S: Paul West & Andrew McCullough
GS: Sarah Marshall (*Amanda*), Dan Tobin (*Felix*), Frank
Maxwell (*Bull Bullock*)
The Stones put their house up for sale, but after
reminiscing about their years there, they change
their minds.

DR274. **"By Line- Jeffrey Stone"**   3/19/66
W: Andrew McCullough   Story by: Jack Raymond
D: Andrew McCullough
GS: Binnie Barnes (*Maddy*), Leslie Gore (*Herself*),
Darryl Richard (*Smitty*), Penny Kunard (*Bettina*)
Jeff and Smitty try to get Leslie Gore, who is
appearing in town, to record their new song.

Radio Appearances

R1. ***STAR & THE STORY***   (4/30/44, WCBS, 30 min.)
     "The Outsider"
     Walter Pidgeon (*Host*), Donna Reed (*Laura Sturdee*)
     The hopelessly crippled daughter of a famous New York
     doctor finds a new life through her faith in an
     unknown healer.

R2. ***SILVER THEATER***   (7/2/44, WCBS, 30 min.)
     "Partners in Blue"
     Donna Reed (*Yeoman Second Class Sally Hayward*)
     A WAVE sets out to find the man she actually released
     for combat duty when she enlisted.

R3. ***SCREEN GUILD THEATER***   (9/4/44, WCBS, 30 min.)
     "Too Many Husbands"
     Frank Sinatra, Donna Reed and Bill Goodwin
     A widow remarries, and then discovers that her first
     husband is not really dead.

R4. ***LUX RADIO THEATRE***   (10/22/45, WCBS, 60 min.)
     "Lost Angel"
     Margaret O'Brien (*Alpha*), George Murphy (*Mike Degan*),
     Donna Reed (*Katie Mallory*)
     A group of scientists use a six-year-old genius as
     the subject for experiments in human behavior.

R5. ***SCREEN GUILD THEATER***   (11/5/45, WABC, 30 min.)
     "Hail, the Conquering Hero"
     Eddie Bracken (*Woodrow Lafayette Pershing Truesmith*),
     Donna Reed (*Libby*), William Demarest
     Preston Sturges' story of a man, rejected by the
     Army, who is mistaken as a war hero by his home town.

R6. ***SCREEN GUILD THEATER***   (8/12/46, WABC, 30 min.)
     "Devil and Miss Jones"
     Van Johnson, Donna Reed (*Mary Jones*), Guy Kibbee
     A millionaire masquerades as a clerk in his own
     department store in order to investigate employee
     complaints.

R7.   ***THE CAVALCADE OF AMERICA***   (2/10/47, WNBC, 30 min.)
      "The Voice of the Wizard"
      Dane Clark (*Thomas Edison*), Donna Reed (*Mary Stilwell Edison*), Alan Hewitt (*Manager*), Robert Dryden (*John Kruesi*), Jack Manning (*Fred*), John Sylvester (*George*), Chester Stratton (*The Reporter*)
      This dramatization of the life of inventor Thomas Edison chronicles his invention of the phonograph and his proposal to future wife Mary- in Morse code!

R8.   ***LUX RADIO THEATRE***   (3/10/47, WCBS, 60 min.)
      "It's a Wonderful Life"
      James Stewart (*George Bailey*), Donna Reed (*Mary Hatch*) and J. Carroll Naish
      This hour long version was the first of several radio adaptations of the film (see F19).

R9.   ***HI, JINX!***   (6/16/47, WNBC, 30 min.)
      Donna and her sister Heidi, a model, appeared on Jinx Falkenburg's morning interview show.

R10. ***SCREEN GUILD PLAYERS***   (12/29/47, WCBS, 30 min.)
      "It's a Wonderful Life"
      James Stewart (*George Bailey*), Donna Reed (*Mary Hatch*), and Victor Moore (*Clarence*)

R11. ***FAMILY THEATER***   (5/13/48, Mutual, 30 min.)
      "Song for a Long Road"
      John Lund, Donna Reed, Glenn Langan

R12. ***LUX RADIO THEATRE***   (6/28/48, WCBS, 60 min.)
      "You Were Meant for Me"
      Dan Dailey (*Chuck Arnold*), Donna Reed (*Peggy Mayhew*)
      A small town girl marries a bandleader during the Depression.

R13. ***LUX RADIO THEATRE***   (9/12/49, WCBS, 60 min.)
      "Deep Waters"
      Dana Andrews (*Hod Stillwell*), Donna Reed (*Ann Freeman*)
      A lobster fisherman adopts a problem orphan boy.

R14. ***SCREEN GUILD PLAYERS***   (12/29/49, WNBC, 30 min.)
      "It's a Wonderful Life"
      James Stewart (*George Bailey*), Donna Reed (*Mary Hatch*), and Victor Moore (*Clarence*)

R15. ***STARS OVER HOLLYWOOD***   (5/13/50, WCBS, 30 min.)
      "Letter from Rio"
      Donna Reed

R16. ***MGM THEATRE OF THE AIR***   (7/21/50, WMGM, 60 min.)
      "My Dear Miss Aldrich"
      Donna Reed (*Martha Aldrich*)

R17. ***FAMILY THEATRE***   (10/25/50, Mutual, 30 min.)
      "Jane Eyre"
      Donna Reed (*Jane Eyre*), Vincent Price (*Rochester*), Tony Lafrano, Irene Tedrow, Ben Wright, Joan Evans
      Radio adaptation of the Charlotte Bronte classic.

R18.   *PAULA STONE'S HOLLYWOOD*   (12/26/50, WMGM, 15 min.)
       Host Paula Stone interviews Donna at home.

R19.   *SCREEN GUILD PLAYERS*   (3/15/51, WABC, 60 min.)
       "It's a Wonderful Life"
       James   Stewart   (*George   Bailey*),   Donna   Reed   (*Mary
       Hatch*), and Victor Moore (*Clarence*)

R20.   *LUX RADIO THEATRE*   (11/26/51, WCBS, 60 min.)
       "To Please a Lady"
       Donna Reed (*Regina Forbes*), Adolphe Menjou (*Gregg*),
       and John Hodiak (*Mike Brannan*)
       A ruthless race car driver falls for the woman
       reporter who has been hounding him.

R21.   *STARS IN THE AIR*   (12/13/51, WCBS, 30 min.)
       "It's a Wonderful Life"
       James   Stewart   (*George   Bailey*),   Donna   Reed   (*Mary
       Hatch*), Joseph Granby, Junius Matthews, Verna Felton
       (*Mrs. Hatch*)

R22.   *MARTIN & LEWIS*   (2/17/53, WNBC, 30 min.)
       Guest on Dean Martin and Jerry Lewis' comedy show.

R23.   *1953 ACADEMY AWARDS*   (3/25/54, WNBC, 2 hours)
       Radio simulcast of the 26th annual Academy Awards
       presentation.   Donna   Reed accepted Best Supporting
       Actress Oscar (see T1).

R24.   *THE BOB HOPE SHOW*   (4/23/54, WNBC, 30 min.)
       Guest appearance in a skit with Bob Hope.

R25.   *LUX RADIO THEATRE*   (6/7/54, WCBS, 60 min.)
       "The Naked Jungle"
       Charlton Heston (*Christopher Leiningen*), Donna Reed
       (*Joanna   Leiningen*),   Jay   Novello   (*Commissioner*),
       hosted by Irving Cummings.
       A woman is married by proxy to a South American cocoa
       planter,   and   when   she   arrives they discover they
       cannot stand one another. He sends her away but
       before she can leave, the plantation is threatened by
       an advancing army of red ants. In the face of
       adversity,   they   pull   together, conquer the insects
       and fall in love.

R26.   *LUX RADIO THEATRE*   (9/28/54, WNBC, 60 min.)
       "How Green Was My Valley"
       Michael Rennie (*Mr. Gruffydd*), Donna Reed (*Angharad*),
       and Donald Crisp (*Mr. Morgan*)
       Story centers on a large family in a Welsh coal
       mining village.

R27.   *EASTER SEAL PARADE OF STARS* (3/10/55, WNBC, 30 min.)
       Variety Show with Dan O'Herlihy, Jeanette McDonald
       Donna Reed speaks on behalf of the National Society
       for Crippled Children and Adults.

R28.   *ANNUAL ALL-STAR RED CROSS SHOW* (3/20/55, WNBC, 30 m.)
       With Jeff Chandler, Barbara Stanwyck, Loretta Young
       Donna appeared in a vignette with Chandler.

R29. *LUX RADIO THEATRE*   (3/22/55, WNBC, 60 min.)
      "Rawhide"
      Jeffrey Hunter (*Tom Owens*), Donna Reed (*Vinnie Holt*),
      William Conrad (*Zimmerman*), Lawrence Dobkin (*Tevis*),
      Jack Kruschen (*Gratz*), hosted by Irving Cummings.
      Two strangers   meet at   a desolate stagecoach station
      in the Old West, and are   held hostage   by an escaped
      criminal.

R30. *CAVALCADE OF STARS*   (3/27/55, WNBC, 30 min.)
      With Cecil B. DeMille, Adolph Zukor, Walt Disney,
      William Holden, Jane Wyman, Mary Pickford, Donna Reed

R31. *1954 ACADEMY AWARDS*   (3/30/55, WNBC, 90 min.)
      Simulcast of the Oscar presentation, with Bob Hope in
      Hollywood   and   Thelma   Ritter   in   New   York.   Donna
      presented the Best Supporting Actor award (See T3).

Awards and Nominations

A1. 1942 "Stars of Tomorrow" Award
Presented annually by Quigley Publications to a
handful of performers "most likely to achieve major
stardom." Among the others named in 1942 were Van
Heflin, Eddie Bracken, Jane Wyman, Alan Ladd and
Betty Hutton.

A2. 1953 Academy Award
Presented by the Academy of Motion Picture Arts and
Sciences on March 25, 1954 at the RKO Pantages
Theater, Hollywood, California.

The nominations for Best Supporting Actress were:
Grace Kelly for _Mogambo_, Geraldine Page for _Hondo_,
Majorie Rambeau for _Torch Song_, Thelma Ritter for
Pickup on South Street, and Donna Reed for _From Here
to Eternity_ (See F28). The envelope please...

When Donna Reed's name was announced by Walter
Brennan, she sprinted down the aisle. Later she said
"I ran? I don't believe it!" (see B71, B261, T1, R23)

Donna's Oscar statuette currently resides at McHenry
House, a historical museum dedicated to the heritage
of Crawford County, Iowa (see B223, B228).

A3. 1958-1959 Emmy nomination
Presented May 6, 1959. Best Actress in a Leading
Role in a Comedy nomination for "The Donna Reed
Show." (See T7). Award went to Jane Wyatt for
"Father Knows Best."

A4. 1959 American Mothers Committee Award
Presented by the American Mothers Committee at their
25th Annual Mothers Convention in May, 1959 (see
B46).

A5.   1959-1960 Emmy nomination
        Presented June   20, 1960.   Outstanding Performance by
        an Actress in a Series.   Nomination for "The Donna
        Reed Show." Award went to Jane Wyatt.

A6.   1960-1961 Emmy nomination
        Presented May 16, 1961. Outstanding Performance by a
        Lead Actress in a Series. Nomination for "The Donna
        Reed Show."   Award went to Barbara Stanwyck for "The
        Barbara Stanwyck Show."

A7.   1961-1962 Emmy nomination
        Presented May 22, 1962.   Outstanding Continued
        Performance by   an Actress in a Series (Lead).
        Nomination for "The Donna Reed Show." Award went to
        Shirley Booth for "Hazel."

A8.   1962 Golden Globe Award   (Hollywood Foreign Press
        Association)
        Best Television Star, Female.

A9.   1964 Golden Apple Award
        Presented by the Hollywood Women's Press Club. As
        "Most Co-operative Star (w/Lorne Greene). Reported
        in the L.A. Times on 12/21/64, photo.

A10.   1964 Women's Auxiliary to the AMA Award
        The Women's   Auxiliary to   the American Medical
        Association presented Donna with this special award
        "because through her TV program she exemplifies the
        ideals and dedication of the doctor's wife in a
        warmly understanding and convincing manner" (See
        B124).

A11.   1965 Genii Award winner
        Presented by Hedda Hopper at the 11th annual banquet
        of the Radio &   Television Women   of Southern
        California, on 5/14/65.   Previous winners: Lucille
        Ball, Barbara Stanwyck, Shirley Booth, Loretta Young.
        Reported in the Hollywood Citizen-News on 5/15/65.

A12.   Hollywood Walk of Fame Star
        The Hollywood Chamber of Commerce recognized Donna
        Reed with a Star on the Walk of Fame, the highest
        honor they can accord a person in the entertainment
        industry. A commemorative plaque was presented to
        the Donna Reed Foundation for the Performing Arts in
        June 1986. Her Star is located at 1612 Vine Street.

A13.   The Donna Reed Foundation for the Performing Arts
        Established in Denision, Iowa in 1986, the Foundation
        is dedicated to the memory of Donna Reed and the
        principles for which she stood: "honesty, integrity
        and commitment to family, community and profession."
        For more information on the Foundation and their
        annual Donna Reed Festival, see the Appendix.

Annotated Bibliography

This bibliography is divided in eight sub-sections. The first five sections cover one decade each of Donna Reed's career. The sixth section lists obituaries, the seventh memorial articles, and the last covers book excerpts.

1940s

B1.   Bangs, Bee.   "There Are No Rules." (So contends Donna Reed, in explaining her success and recent promotion to stardom.) _Silver Screen_, May 1946, p. 48-49+.

A portrait of a generous, unassuming and wise actress. Her background is discussed, up to her role in "Faithful in My Fashion." (see F18)

B2.   "Campus Queen Comes to Hollywood." _The Lion's Roar_, January 1942.

(_The Lion's Roar_ was Metro-Goldwyn-Mayer's studio magazine.)

B3.   "Cinderella Has No Cinch." _The Lion's Roar_, September 1943.

B4.   "Corn-fed Beauty." _The Lion's Roar_, April 1942.

B5.   "Design for Stardom." _The Lion's Roar_, July 1943.

B6.   "Directors' Actress." _The Lion's Roar_, Vol. IV, 1945.

B7.   "Divorce Won by Donna Reed." _Los Angeles Times_, January 13, 1945.

Brief article   regarding Donna's divorce from Bill
Tuttle, from whom   she   had   been   separated since
December 3, 1944.

B8.   "Donna Mullenger Becomes Donna Adams, Screen Star."
       Denison Review (Denison, Iowa), May 1, 1941, p. 1.

       Feature with photo announces Donna's name change
       and contract with MGM.   Donna says "Whew! I'm
       still in a daze."

B9.   "Donna Reed: James Stewart's new leading lady spends
       a weekend in a small town." Life, June 10, 1946,
       p. 133-6 (also cover photo).

       In order to 're-indoctrinate' her in small town
       life, the press agents for It's A Wonderful Life
       sent Donna to Saratoga, California.   Photos show
       her visiting the fix-it shop, and Main Street, and
       chatting with townspeople.

B10.   "Donna Reed Weds."   Los Angeles Herald-Examiner,
       March 1, 1943.

       Re: wedding of Donna Reed and William Tuttle.

B11.   "Donna Up to Date." The Lion's Roar, 1946.

       Includes quotes by director John Ford, regarding
       her work on They Were Expendable (see F17).

B12.   Evening Public Ledger, June 17, 1941, photo.

       A photograph of 20 year old Donna Reed, announcing
       her $75/week contract with MGM.

B13.   "Go West(ern) Young Lady."   The Lion's Roar, Volume
       II, 1943-44, 2 pp.

       Donna discusses a "new experience": westerns,
       Gentle Annie in particular (see F15).

B14.   Hamilton,   Sara.   "Round-up of Pace Setters."
       Photoplay, October 1942, p. 51+.

       Biographical sketches of Leif Erickson, Irene
       Manning, Jack Carson and Donna Reed.

B15.   Hardy, Spencer.   "Farm Girl Donna's Still On The 6
       A.M. Shift- Even in Hollywood."   New York Daily
       Mirror, March 16, 1947, p. 5.

       Brief article compares the life of the star in
       Hollywood to her earlier life back on the farm.

B16.   "Her First Year." The Lion's Roar, September/October
       1942.

B17.   Holliday, K.   "Farmer's Daughter."   Colliers, June
       27, 1942, p. 13+.

B18.   "Homespun." <u>American Magazine</u>, September 1942, p. 71.

        Brief article states that Denison, Iowa had
        recently celebrated 'Mullenger Day' in her honor.

B19.   Howe, Herb. "Wonderful Life with Donna." <u>Photoplay</u>,
        July 1947, p. 64-65, 87-88.

        Article recounts Donna Reed and Tony Owen's
        courtship, gives background information on Owen,
        and includes photos of Donna with sister Karen.

B20.   "Into Movies." <u>Denison Review</u> (Iowa), April 10, 1941.

        Small article announces that Donna Mullenger of
        Denison received a contract with MGM, and a role
        in "Enemy Within" (early title for <u>The Get-Away</u>.)
        States that her agents are considering 'Donna
        Denison' as her screen name.

B21.   "Iowa Corn to Cinema Queen- Donna's Done It!"
        <u>Milwaukee Journal</u>, January 18, 1942, p. 3.

        Full page article details Donna's background, from
        the farm to her fourth film, <u>The Bugle Sounds</u>.

B22.   Johnson, Erskine. "Drama Born of School Days." <u>New
        York World-Telegram</u>, 'In Hollywood' column,
        February 13, 1946.

        Dr. Edward Tompkins (see T6), Donna's chemistry
        teacher from Denison, is appointed technical
        adviser on MGM film <u>The Beginning of the End</u>
        thanks to correspondence with Donna.

B23.   "Judy Garland, Donna Reed Become Brides; Film
        Newlyweds Leave on their Honeymoons." <u>Los Angeles
        Times</u>, June 16, 1945, p. 3.

        Article states that the two actresses were married
        on the same day. (Judy Garland to Vincent
        Minnelli, Donna Reed to Tony Owen.) The two
        couples then left on the same train to their
        honeymoon destinations.

B24.   "The Life Story of Donna Reed." <u>Picture Show</u>
        (London), July 29, 1944, p. 11.

B25.   <u>Los Angeles Times</u>, December 2, 1940.

        Donna's photo appeared with announcement that she
        had been named Campus Queen at L.A. City College.

B26.   Metro-Goldwyn-Mayer Biographical Information Sheet.
        Completed by Donna Reed, dated April 5, 1941.
        Located at the Academy of Motion Picture Arts and
        Sciences Library, Hollywood, California.

B27.   "On the Star Trail." <u>The Lion's Roar</u>, March 1942.

B28.   Parsons, Louella O.   "Cosmopolitan's Citation For
        Best Performance of Month."   Cosmopolitan
        Magazine, January 1947, p. 66.

B29.   Parsons, Louella O.   "Donna Reed, Husband Part:
        Neither will talk except to say marriage has
        failed."   Los Angeles Herald-Examiner, December
        13, 1944.

B30.   Parsons, Louella O. "Donna Reed Wins Divorce Decree
        in Juarez." Los Angeles Herald-Examiner, Jan. 13,
        1945.

B31.   Redelings, Lowell E.   "An Actress Talks About
        Washington." Hollywood Scene column. Hollywood
        Citizen-News, January 7, 1946, p. 6.

B32.   Schallert, Edwin.   "Donna Reed Hailed as 'Crown
        Princess.'"   Los Angeles Times, March 26, 1944,
        Part III.

B33.   "School for Glamour." The Lion's Roar, 1941-1942.

B34.   Service, Faith. "Can An Average Girl Succeed In the
        Movies?" Silver Screen, November 1943, p. 24-25+.

        This article compares the lives and lifestyles of
        four young actresses- Donna Reed, Susan Peters,
        Teresa Wright, and Nancy Coleman. All four
        "ordinary, sensible" stars are given equal space,
        but Donna is singled out as the "prettiest of the
        four girls".

B35.   Service, Faith. "What's Happened to Donna?" Silver
        Screen, December 1947, p. 43.

        Donna answers the reporter's question, "Happiness
        is what has happened to me."

B36.   Skolsky, Sidney. "No Bad Habits." Hollywood Is My
        Beat column.   New York Post Week-End Magazine,
        December 6, 1947, p. 12

B37.   "Small, Terrific and Corn-Fed." Photoplay and Movie
        Mirror, October 1942.

B38.   Stanley, Fred.   "Hollywood's Films Follow Our Battle
        Flags; Metro Prepares 'Dragon Seed.'"   New York
        Times, August 22, 1943.

        Regarding the making of Pearl S. Buck's novel.
        Donna Reed, Van Heflin, Greer Garson, Hedy Lamarr
        and Edward G. Robinson, among others, tested for
        roles but did not look "sufficiently Oriental."

B39.   "Stars of Tomorrow." The Lion's Roar, August 1942.

B40.   "Sweetheart of the Army."   The Lion's Roar, April
        1944.

B41. Wilkinson, Lupton A. "Movie Meanie...But Audiences
      Know Donna Reed's Really Nice. Watch Them..."
      This Week, November 8, 1942, p. 14.

      Title refers to her role as the "hateful step-
      daughter" in Eyes In The Night. Article relates
      how she won a $50 war bond from Lionel Barrymore
      when he bet she couldn't really milk a cow.

B42. Wilson, C. "Cinderella--Believe It Or Not." The
      Lion's Roar, July/August 1942.

                        1950s

B43. Bender, Harold. "The Donna Reed Show: A Family
      Affair." Pictorial TView, January 25, 1959, p. 14.

B44. Berg, Louis. "Don't Look At Donna!" Los Angeles
      Herald Examiner, February 26, 1956. (Syndicated
      piece which also appeared in the same day's New
      York Herald-Tribune.)

      Short item with candid photos of Donna in curlers.

B45. Brownell, William H., Jr. "The Way to 'Eternity':
      Donna Reed Reflects on Past and Prize Roles." New
      York Times, April 25, 1954, p. X5.

B46. Chapman, Priscilla. "Donna Reed Wins Citation for
      Television Family Show." New York Herald Tribune,
      May 20, 1959.

      Donna was presented an award from the American
      Mother's Committee (the founders of Mother's Day)
      at their 25th annual Mother's Convention (see A4).

B47. Churchill, Reba and Bonnie. "Would Like to Co-Star
      With Kirk Douglas." Hollywood Diary column.
      Beverly Hills News Life, December 10, 1953.

      In this item in the "Hollywood Diary" column,
      Donna expressed her wish to co-star with Douglas
      in Heaven Knows Mr. Allison. (The roles went to
      Robert Mitchum and Deborah Kerr.)

B48. "Donna's Brood." Silver Screen, October 1956.

      Picture feature.

B49. "Donna Does It, Sponsor Says." Variety, April 8,
      1959.

      Recalls the shaky start of "The Donna Reed Show."

B50.   "Donna Reed Faces Surgery." <u>New York Times</u>, January 6, 1955.

Brief item states that she entered St. John's Hospital in Santa Monica for "minor surgery."

B51.   "Donna Reed In Denison On Visit." <u>The Denison Bulletin</u> (Denison, Iowa), January 28, 1955, p. 1.

This front page article includes a photo of Donna kissing her grandmother, Mary Mullenger, on the latter's 91st birthday.

B52.   "Donna Reed Set as Mrs. Sigmund Romberg." <u>Los Angeles Times</u>, March 29, 1954.

Brief item stating that Donna would be playing the role in <u>Deep in My Heart</u>. (She did not.)

B53.   Goldsmith, B.   "My Most Wonderful Time of Day." <u>Woman's Home Companion</u>, February 1956, p. 18-20.

B54.   Gross, Ben.   "Movie Gals Have A Better Chance In TV-Donna Reed." <u>New York Sunday News</u>, October 12, 1958, Section II, p. 27-30.

B55.   Hale, Wanda.   "Eternal Campus Queen Is Bad Girl in Eternity." <u>New York Sunday News</u>, August 23, 1953, Section II, page 6.

After years of playing sweet ingenues, Donna Reed wanted to test her ability in a dramatic role as a "bad girl." The opportunity came with <u>From Here to Eternity</u>.

B56.   Hall, Gladys.   "What Is This Thing Called Love?" <u>Photoplay</u>, July 1955, p. 46-47+.

B57.   Hopper, Hedda.   "The Benny Goodman Story: Donna Reed Helps Hollywood Tell A Chicago Story." <u>Chicago Tribune Magazine</u>, November 13, 1955, p. 26-27.

B58.   Hopper, Hedda.   "Donna Reed Has New Daughter." <u>Los Angeles Times</u>, May 8, 1957.

B59.   Hopper, Hedda.   "Only Tantrums Donna Throws Are In Films: Demure Miss Reed Has Punch." <u>Los Angeles Times</u>, November 13, 1955.

Basically the same article as B57 above, presented with a different slant.

B60.   Humphrey, Hal.   "Donna Is Not All-Out For Togetherness." <u>L.A. Mirror News</u>, May 25, 1959, Part II, p. 6.

Humphrey's profile of Donna is that of a sensible, sweet and devoted wife. Title refers to Donna's opinion that togetherness can be overdone.

B61.   Hyams,   Joe.   "Donna   Reed   in   Africa   Film   to be
        Produced By Husband."   New York Herald Tribune,
        March 25, 1955.

        Brief piece regarding Donna being cast in The Mark
        of the Leopard, later titled Beyond Mombasa (see
        F38).

B62.   Hyams, Joe. "Donna Reed Is Back, Loved Africa." New
        York Herald Tribune, June 6, 1956, p. 15.

B63.   Hyams,   Joe.   "In The News" column.   Hollywood
        Citizen-News, March 29, 1954.

        Re: Deep In My Heart & Last Time I Saw Paris.

B64.   "Just What the Doctor Ordered." TV Guide, December
        13, 1958, p. 8-11.

        During "The Donna Reed Show's" first season, Donna
        questions how well her series will stand up
        against Milton Berle in the ratings.

B65.   Knowles, Melita.   "Star Ends Safari."   Christian
        Science Monitor, May 1, 1956, p. 12.

        The rigors of shooting Beyond Mombasa in Africa.

B66.   Manners, Dorothy.   "Donna Reed's A Country Girl Who
        Made the Glamour Grade."   Los Angeles Examiner,
        Entertainment Magazine, November 28, 1954, p. 3+.

B67.   McClay,   Howard.   "Donna Reed Headed For New
        Horizons." L.A. Daily News, December 3, 1954.

        Regarding her role in Far Horizons (see F34).

B68.   McManus, Margaret. "City Girl Now."   Newark Evening
        News, January 11, 1959.

B69.   "Milestones." Time Magazine, May 20, 1957, p. 122.
        Birth announcement of Donna's daughter, Mary Anne.

B70.   Minoff,   Philip.   TV   personality   profile.
        Everywoman's Family Circle, June 1959, p. 16+.

B71.   Modern Screen, June 1954.
        A piece on the Academy Awards ceremony includes a
        photo of Donna just after winning. States that she
        burst into tears in the press room, and didn't
        remember running down the aisle to receive award.

B72.   Mosby, Aline.   "Donna Reed Calls Africa a
        Honeymooner's Haven." New York World- Telegram
        and Sun, June 12, 1956, p. 15.

        Short article relating to Donna and Tony Owen's
        trip to Africa, where they went to make a film for
        their production company.

B73.   "Never Argue With A Woman: As Donna Reed has proved,
        it seldom pays." TV Guide, August 8, 1959, p. 8-
        11.

B74.   "New Donna Reed Series Set for Bow in Mexico."
        Variety, March 11, 1959.

        Announces plans for "The Donna Reed Show" to be
        dubbed and shown in Mexico under the title "Mama
        Lo Sabe Todo" (Mother Knows Best).

B75.   New York Post, August 7, 1956.

        Photo of Donna Reed and Tony Owen, "who have just
        formed their own production company."

B76.   "On the Cover..." New York Sunday News, Coloroto
        Magazine, February 5, 1956, p. 2 & cover.

B77.   Pam, Jerry. "Can't Leave Donna Out of Top Rating."
        Beverly Hills News Life, March 9, 1954.

        Two weeks before the ceremony, the author
        speculates on Donna's chances of winning an
        Academy Award.

B78.   Parsons, Louella. "Donna Reed, Mate Expect 4th
        Child." Los Angeles Examiner, December 20, 1956.

B79.   Parsons, Louella. "Donna Reed Says Bye-Bye to Goodie-
        Goodie Roles." Pictorial Review, May 9, 1954.

        Interviewed by Louella Parsons after her Oscar
        win, Donna discusses her film beginnings and
        concludes "this is my year."

B80.   Parsons, Louella. "Fun Is A Family Affair For
        Donna." Los Angeles Examiner, September 2, 1956,
        Pictorial Living section, p. 12.

B81.   "Pro Sacajawea." New York Times, April 3, 1955.

        Brief article about Donna Reed's campaign to have
        Sacajawea elected to the Hall of Fame. Donna
        portrayed the Indian woman in The Far Horizons.

B82.   Pryor, Thomas M. "New Metro Role for Donna Reed:
        Oscar Winner signed to do 'Deep In My Heart' after
        completion of 'Paris.'" New York Times, March 29,
        1954.

B83.   Reed, Donna. "Every Day Is Mother's Day- For Donna
        Reed, at least, and here's why." New York Mirror
        Magazine, May 10, 1959, p. 7. cover story.

B84.   Reed, Donna. "The Role I Liked Best..." Saturday
        Evening Post, March 10, 1951.

        The role Donna discusses is that of Marguerite
        Patourel in Green Dolphin Street (see F20).

B85.   Shepard, Richard F. "Star on a Campaign." New York
        Times, November 1, 1959.

        The "campaign" was a publicity tour for "The Donna
        Reed Show's" second season.

B86.   Skolsky, Sidney. "Hard Worker." Hollywood Is My Beat
        column. New York Post, November 22, 1953, p. 5M.

B87.   Skolsky, Sidney. "Tintypes." Hollywood Is My Beat
        column. Hollywood Citizen-News, March 24, 1955.

B88.   Thomas, Bob.   "It's Oscar Time- Wednesday is the Big
        Day." New York Sunday News, March 27, 1955, p. 80.

        Includes a photo of presenter Donna Reed looking
        over the supply of Oscar statuettes.

B89.   Tildesley, Alice L.   "Tips From A Shady Lady."
        Silver Screen, December 1953, p. 38-39; 56-57.

B90.   Van Horne, Harriet.   "Finds Miss Reed Is Nobody's
        Fool." New York World- Telegram and Sun, December
        31, 1958.

        This haughty reporter did   not   anticipate liking
        Donna, as she found "The Donna Reed Show" to be a
        "bleary bit of blanc-mange....indescribably bad."
        However, after being coerced into meeting the
        star, found her to be surprisingly bright, well-
        spoken, and astonishingly pretty.

B91.   Wilson, Earl.   "That's Earl" column. Newark News
        (New Jersey), December 17, 1958.

        Earl and Donna discuss Christmas and hard times
        back on the farm. Syndicated column.

B92.   Wilson, Keith.   "Crawford County's Most Famous
        Citizen." Omaha World-Herald, September 16, 1951.

                              1960s

B93.   "A Lot of Dog for Donna." Life, Aug. 4, 1961, p. 47.

        Photo with Donna and Coco, the 138 pound poodle
        signed for "The Donna Reed Show."

B94.   "At Home With Donna Reed." New York Sunday News,
        December 9, 1962, p. 10.

        One page picture feature has five photos of Donna
        and her real family at home. Donna in the kitchen,
        helping daughter Penny style her hair, etc.

B95.   "At Home With Donna Reed."   <u>New York Sunday News</u>,
        November 29, 1964, p. 17.

        The same format as B94- 5 photos two years later.

B96.   Beck, Marilyn.   "Donna Reed: Men! You Can't Live
        With Them, You Can't Live Without Them!"   <u>TV and
        Movie Screen</u>, March 1966, p. 32-35, 52-54.

        In this article, which features several photos of
        Donna, husband Tony Owen, and daughter Penny, she
        complains about men (particularly Owen) and their
        infuriating ways. In the end, she atones for any
        potential damage her statements may make by
        saying, "Life might not be as frustrating without
        Tony- but it certainly wouldn't be as much fun."

B97.   Christy, George.   "It's Worth Fighting to Save a
        Marriage." <u>Photoplay</u>, February 1960, p. 54-55+.

        Though the title of this article implies that her
        marriage to Tony Owen was in trouble, the piece
        itself is a portrait of a happy marriage that
        endured- with some give and take.

B98.   Denton, Charles.   "A Good Girl Makes Good: Donna
        Reed." <u>Los Angeles Examiner TV Weekly</u>, March 12,
        1961.

B99.   Dern, Marian.   "Sweet, Sincere and Solvent." <u>TV
        Guide</u>, June 20, 1964, p. 10-13, cover.

        The writer compares the Donna Reed Legend to the
        real Donna Reed. Title of the article refers to
        the way Jack Lemmon introduced her on the Oscar
        broadcast that year (see T9).

B100.   "Donna Loses $25,000 Jewels to Thief." (AP) <u>New York
        Daily News</u>, November 26, 1962.

        After spending the Thanksgiving holiday in Palm
        Springs, Donna and her family returned to find
        $25,000 in jewelry missing.

B101.   "Donna Reed (Star of ABC-TV's "The Donna Reed Show.")
        <u>ABC Biography</u>, 1964-65. Located at the New York
        Public Library at Lincoln Center, Theatre
        Collection. Basic press release bio.

B102.   "Donna Reed." <u>Limelight</u>, June 29, 1961. (profile)

B103.   "Donna Reed, Durable Star, Is Still The Girl Next
        Door." <u>Los Angeles Mirror</u>, May 5, 1961, p. II-2.

B104.   "Donna Reed Departs; With a tear... and a smile..."
        <u>TV Guide</u>, March 19, 1966, p. 20-21.

B105.   "Donna Reed's Big TV Plans."   <u>New York Morning
        Telegraph</u>, February 23, 1960.

Donna relates her decision not to continue with her series for more than another two years, after which she would like to produce other projects along with husband Tony.

B106. "The Farmer's Daughter Who Went to Town." *TV Guide,* May 6, 1961, p. 12-15, cover story.

B107. Freeman, Donald. "Donna Reed: Fire and Ice; TV's ranking wife and mother offers some chilly opinions about Hollywood." *Saturday Evening Post,* March 28, 1964, p. 22-23.

Donna's sounds off on Hollywood ("a walled-in city bounded on all sides by arrogance"), directors ("hackneyed craftsmen" who "hate women") and other topics.

B108. "From 'Eternity' To Here." *Newsweek,* July 31, 1961, p. 75.

B109. Gardella, Kay. "Donna Recalls Shaky Start of Her Hit TVer." *New York Sunday News,* May 15, 1960, sec. 2, p. 18.

B110. Gehman, Richard. "Indestructible Donna: She goes on and on, making a success of playing "Nice girls"- but look out!" *The American Weekly Magazine,* January 7, 1962, p. 6-7. (Syndicated magazine, appeared in newspapers nationwide.)

B111. Hannah, Marilyn. "Carl Betz: The Lie He Lived for Eight Years." *TV and Movie Screen,* June 1968, p. 40+.

Donna's TV husband claims to be nothing like the always smiling and patient Dr. Stone.

B112. Humphrey, Hal. "Donna Reed Giddy Over Her Nielsen." *Los Angeles Times,* November 28, 1963, p. V-2.

B113. Humphrey, Hal. "Donna Reed Square? Never." *Los Angeles Times, Weekly TV Magazine,* May 30, 1965.

A rebuttal to all of the then-popular Donna Reed jokes being made by comedians and talk show hosts.

B114. Humphrey, Hal. "Mom Knows Best- Donna To Quit." (Will definitely turn in her TV mother badge next season.) *Los Angeles Times,* July 4, 1962.

Despite this announcement, Donna continued in her role for four more seasons.

B115. Hyams, Joe. "'Tiger' Is Shining Bright." *New York Herald Tribune,* April 9, 1961, Lively Arts Sec.

Donna, as this profile reveals, was nicknamed 'Tiger' because of her determination.

B116.   Judge, Frank. "TV Ribbing That Hurts." <u>Detroit News</u>
        <u>TV Magazine</u>, July 25-31, 1965, cover story, p.4.

B117.   Lamberto, Nick. "Donna Reed: A Mother for Peace."
        <u>Des Moines Sunday Register</u>, July 28, 1968, p. 6-7.

B118.   Lardine, Bob. "It's Still A Man's World." <u>New York</u>
        <u>Sunday News</u>, August 13, 1961, p. 7.

        This reporter observed that of the handful of
        series during the 1960-61 season with women stars,
        all but "The Donna Reed Show" had been cancelled,
        and lets Donna and other female TV stars tell
        their sides.

B119.   Mackin, Tom. "Betz to Play Hot Lawyer." <u>Newark</u>
        <u>Evening News</u>, May 21, 1967.

        In this piece concerning Carl Betz' starring role
        in "Judd for the Defense," he discusses his
        feelings regarding his backseat role in "The Donna
        Reed Show."

B120.   Mackin, Tom. "Donna Dazzles Them: ABC Series In Top
        Ten." <u>Newark Evening News</u>, December 8, 1963.

        Donna's thoughts on why "The Donna Reed Show" is
        high in ratings after six years ("isn't it a
        kick?") and why she doesn't do guest appearances.

B121.   MacMinn, Aleene. "Donna Reed: Producer." <u>Los</u>
        <u>Angeles Times, Weekly TV Magazine</u>, May 27, 1962.

        Donna firmly states that the next (fifth) season
        of "The Donna Reed Show" will be her last, and
        that she would then like to produce comedy films.

B122.   Nichols, M. "Farmer's Daughter." <u>Coronet</u>, February
        1960, p. 14.

B123.   "No Prima Donna." <u>TV Guide</u>, March 26, 1960, p. 24-
        26, cover story.

        Donna looks back at the first eighteen months of
        "The Donna Reed Show".

B124.   Peters, Ann. "Real Life For the Doctor's Wife."
        <u>Today's Health</u>, June 1964, p. 24-25+.

        This article explores how realistic TV shows ("The
        Donna Reed Show" in particular) which portray the
        lives of doctors' wives are. Donna is photographed
        with real life doctor's wives, and comments on her
        show.

B125.   Pratt, George. "Donna Reed's Day Much Like Yours."
        <u>Hollywood Citizen-News</u>, February 17, 1961, p. 1,6.

B126.   Reed, Donna. "I'm Through Being Bad!" <u>Women's</u>
        <u>World</u>, September 1965, p. 119-120.

Guest columnist Donna Reed discloses that she wouldn't take another role like that of Alma in *From Here to Eternity* if it would make her family uncomfortable.

B127. Reed, Donna. "My Children Love Me Because I'm Strict!: This famous actress reveals her approach to parenthood; though it's old-fashioned, it seems startlingly new in an age when psychology books rule most roosts." *Family Weekly*, March 27, 1960, p. 8, 16.

B128. "Rob Home of Donna Reed." *Los Angeles Herald-Examiner*, November 26, 1962, p. B-8.

The home of Donna Reed and Tony Owen, at 702 N. Alpine Drive in Beverly Hills, was looted during their Thanksgiving vacation. $25,000 worth of property was stolen.

B129. Salmaggi, Bob. "Honesty: The Better Part of Ratings." *New York Herald Tribune*, October 23, 1960, p. 60-62.

B130. "Settles Out of Court With Film Studio." *New York Daily News*, July 5, 1963.

Brief UPI piece about the $70,192 suit Donna filed against Universal Pictures Co. over her 1956 contract. The amount of the settlement is not disclosed.

B131. Stein, Herb. "Owen, Donna Reed A Happy Couple In TV and at Home." Hollywood column. *New York Morning Telegraph*, August 16, 1961.

Background on Tony Owen, and his speculations on the success of "The Donna Reed Show." First of two parts.

B132. Stein, Herb. "Owen Attributes Success to Luck- Tells How TV Show Has Become Popular." Hollywood column. *New York Morning Telegraph*, August 17, 1961.

A continuation of B131 above.

B133. "They Love Donna Even If Emmy Ignores Her." *Los Angeles Times*, September 6, 1964, Calendar section.

B134. Thomas, Bob. "Donna Reed Heaves A Big Sigh of Relief." *New York Post*, December 23, 1965.

An interview with Donna on the last day of filming for "The Donna Reed Show." She discusses the changes in the series over the years, and her reluctance to act again.

B135.   Turmell,   Kitte.   "Family Holiday with Donna Reed."
        Los Angeles Times, Home Magazine, December 24,
        1961.

B136.   "Two Interpretations of the Inner Court." Los Angeles
        Times, Home Magazine, May 3, 1964, p. 30-31.

        Photos of Donna Reed's patio.

B137.   Reed, Donna.   "What Greater Service?" NEA Journal
        (National Education Association of the U.S.),
        January 1963, p. 29.

        In this guest editorial, Donna speaks her opinions
        on the state of education in the United States.
        Photo with her son Tony, in his classroom.

B138.   "Wheeling and Dealing- Hollywood Style." TV Guide,
        July 21, 1962, p. 18-21, cover story.

                            1970s

B139.   "Actress, Writer Propose Peace Day for Mothers."
        Hollywood Citizen-News, April 25, 1970.

B140.   "Donna Reed Divorced."   The Toronto Telegram, June
        10, 1971, p. 63.

B141.   "Donna Reed Leads a Group of Mothers Who Want
        Answers." Coronet, July 1971, p. 12-17.

B142.   "Donna Talks of Then and Now."   New York Daily News,
        January 11, 1979, p. 107.

B143.   Dye, Lee. "Initiative to Put Curbs on Atom Plants
        Started." Los Angeles Times, March 12, 1974, Part
        II, p. 1.

        Donna voices her opinion on behalf of "Another
        Mother for Peace."

B144.   Edison, Robert.   "A Movie Buff's Guide to Who's Not
        Who." New York Times, November 9, 1975.

        A brief piece about actors who have changed their
        names.

B145.   Gardella, Kay. "It's Back to Television..."   New
        York Daily News, May 25, 1979.

        Brief piece in Kay Gardella's column regarding
        "The Best Place to Be" (see T10) and Donna's long
        absence from television.

B146. Hamilton,   J.   "Where   Oh   Where   Are the Beautiful
       Girls." Look, November 3, 1970, p. 67.

       A "Whatever Became Of..." type article.

B147. Handsaker, Gene. "Donna Reed's New Life."   New York
       Post, March 27, 1971.

       Donna speaks about her activities with "Another
       Mother for Peace," and states that serving the
       cause of peace is "everything" to her.

B148. Lewis, Dan.   "Shelly Fabares is Coming Back at Ripe
       Old Age of 28." Boston Sunday Herald Advertiser,
       February 11, 1973, p. 16.

       Donna's television daughter discusses the close
       relationship she shares with her "Donna Reed Show"
       castmates.

B149. "N-Plant Recheck   Urged."   Los   Angeles Herald-
       Examiner, December 9, 1975.

       Donna Reed speaks as President of "Another Mother
       for Peace."   Urges monitoring of nuclear power
       plant in California.

B150. Osborne, Robert. "On Location" column.   Hollywood
       Reporter, August 2, 1977.

B151. Osborne, Robert.   "On Location" column. Hollywood
       Reporter, December 29, 1978.

       Donna discusses her return to television and her
       role in "The Best Place to Be" (see T10).

B152. Osborne, Robert.   "Reed   Between   the Lines."
       Sundancer, October 1977.

B153. Porter, Thomas.   "'Donna Reed Show' Making TV
       Comeback- As a Movie."   The National Enquirer,
       October 1971.

       Paul Petersen talks about a planned TV movie
       reuniting "The Donna Reed Show" cast, for which he
       wrote the screenplay. The film was never made.

B154. Rosenberg, Howard. "Anywhere Else Is 'Best Place to
       Be.'" Los Angeles Times, May 26, 1979.

       An article/review regarding Donna's TV comeback in
       "The Best Place to Be" (see T10).

B155. Willens, Michelle. "Miss Reed Starring for Peace."
       Los Angeles Times, May 6, 1971.

1980s

B156. Beck, Marilyn. <u>New York Daily News</u>, April 16, 1985, p. 81.

In her column, Beck reports that Lorimar president Lee Rich asserted that "Dallas" retained its 40 Nielsen share during Donna's run, and that cruel reports to the contrary were unfounded.

B157. Brown, Meredith. "Mother Knows Best." <u>Soap Opera Digest</u>, February 12, 1985, p. 116-19, 133.

B158. Chapman, Mike. "Donna Reed: Movie Star from Denison." ("Iowans of Impact") <u>Iowa REC News</u>, February, 1984, p. 10-11.

B159. "Donna Reed Ill With Cancer." <u>New York Times</u>, December 22, 1985, p. L23.

B160. "Donna Reed Lassos a Role on 'Dallas.'" <u>USA Today</u>, June 6, 1984, p. 2D.

This item on the People page reported that Donna would be joining the cast of 'Dallas' and contradicted rumors that Mary Martin was being considered for the role.

B161. "Donna Reed Loses Bid for 'Dallas' Role." <u>New York Times</u>, June 19, 1985, p. C21.

B162. "Donna Reed Loves New 'Dallas' Role." (UPI) <u>Los Angeles Times</u>, June 14, 1984.

B163. Esterly, Glenn. "The New Miss Ellie Isn't Afraid to Back J.R. Against The Wall." <u>TV Guide</u>, November 24, 1984, p. 43-48.

B164. Farber, Stephen. "The Role Is Familiar, But the Face..." <u>New York Times</u>, November 4, 1984, sec. 2, p. 27.

Article discusses what happens when one performer replaces another in a role. Donna's "Dallas" role is used as the main example.

B165. Gardella, Kay. "Offscreen With the New Miss Ellie." <u>New York Daily News</u>, July 12, 1984, p. 86.

B166. Green, Michelle and David Wallace. "As Dallas' New Miss Ellie, Donna Reed Trades the Kitchen for a Home on the Range." <u>People Magazine</u>, November 19, 1984, p. 91-4.

B167. Green, Tom. "Donna Reed: Mom For All TV Seasons." <u>USA Today</u>, November 8, 1984.

B168. Holley, David. "Reed Loses Bid to Block 'Dallas.'" <u>Los Angeles Times</u>, June 19, 1985.

B169. Horning, Jay. "Donna Reed: From Champion Biscuit Maker to Fighter for Peace." St. Petersburg Times [St. Petersburg, Florida], March 21, 1982.

B170. Jahr, Cliff. "Great Hollywood Comebacks; Anne Baxter, Jane Wyman, Donna Reed- are back, in nighttime soaps." Ladies Home Journal, June 1985, p. 58-65+.

B171. Lewis, Jerry D. "With Family Grown, Actress Working Again." Grit, September 30, 1984, p. 3.

B172. "Little Miss Ellie Is Fit To Be Tied: Sues For $7-Million." Variety, May 29, 1985, p. 134.

B173. MacTrevor, J. "'Dallas' lui offre un million de dollars pour s'en aller!" Cine Revue (Belgium), May 9, 1985, p. 50-51.

Rough translation: "Dallas" offers her one million dollars to walk away.

B174. MacTrevor, J. "L'etonnant proces qui menace 'Dallas!'" Cine Revue, June 20, 1985, p. 6-7.

An interview with photographs. Relating to Donna's "astonishing lawsuit" against 'Dallas' producers.

B175. Mallory, Bob. "Jubilant Donna Reed Says Her $1.25M Victory Over Dallas Bosses Soothes Her Anger About Firing." Star, September 3, 1985, p. 10.

B176. Marlow, Shirley. "Newsmakers." Los Angeles Times, May 26, 1985.

Regarding lawsuit against "Dallas" producers.

B177. Morrison, Mark. "Dallas' New Miss Ellie." Us Magazine, November 19, 1984, p. 18-21.

B178. "New Miss Ellie Paid Her Dues As 'Mom.'" New York Post, February 1, 1985, p. 9.

B179. Osborne, Robert. "Rambling Reporter" column. Hollywood Reporter, May 29, 1985.

Regarding the cruel and unfair treatment of Donna Reed by Lorimar and CBS Entertainment, and her subsequent lawsuit.

B180. Osborne, Robert. "Rambling Reporter" column. Hollywood Reporter, August 20, 1985.

Donna calls her settlement with "Dallas" producers "very fair and quite generous".

B181. "Pancreatic Cancer Strikes Donna Reed; Condition is 'Good.'" Daily Variety, December 23, 1985.

B182.   Pollock, Jim.   "Donna Does 'Dallas': Nephew says actress bored with retirement." <u>Des Moines Sunday Register</u>, June 24, 1984, p. 4-TV.

The writer interviews residents of Denison, including Donna's brother and nephew, regarding her return to TV.

B183.   "Reed Leaving Hospital." <u>Variety</u>, December 25, 1985, p. 4.

B184.   "Reed Likely to Leave Cedars-Sinai Today." <u>Daily Variety</u>, December 24, 1985.

Her manager, Harry Flynn, said "she is feeling fine."

B185.   Rhein, Dave.   "Donna Does 'Dallas': Iowan Reed takes role of Miss Ellie." <u>Des Moines Sunday Register</u>, June 24, 1984, p. 4-TV.

Interview with Donna regarding her return to television, and her activities during her retirement.

B186.   Rothenberg, Fred.   "Donna Reed Makes the Move to 'Dallas'." <u>Los Angeles Times</u>, August 31, 1984, Part VI, p. 22.

B187.   Scott, Vernon.   "The New Miss Ellie Will Just Show Up." <u>San Francisco Chronicle</u>, September 3, 1984, p. 36.

B188.   Seligson, Tom.   "Everybody's Mom?" <u>Parade Magazine</u>, February 3, 1985, p. 4-7 & cover.

In this in-depth interview, Donna discusses her marriages, children and forty years in show business.

B189.   Smith, Liz.   <u>New York Daily News</u>, April 18, 1985, p. 10.

This item in Liz Smith's column reports "don't feel too sorry for Donna Reed...she'll get a neat $1 million for doing absolutely nothing."

B190.   Wisehart, Bob.   "Donna Reed Nervous Over 'Dallas' Role." <u>Sunday Omaha Journal and Star</u>, June 24, 1984, p. 1TV+.

Obituaries

B191.   "Actress Donna Reed Dies of Pancreatic Cancer at 64." <u>Omaha World-Herald</u>, January 15, 1986, p. 49.

B192. Arar, Yardena. "TV Star Donna Reed Dies of Cancer." *L.A. Life, Daily News*, January 15, 1986, p. 16.

B193. Bianculli, David. "Actress Donna Reed; Oscar Winner and Star of '60s Television Show." *Philadelphia Inquirer*, January 15, 1986, p. 6B.

B194. Burgess, Patricia. "Donna Reed." *The Annual Obituary 1986*, Chicago: St. James Press, 1989, p. 64-65.

B195. Clark, Mike and Monica Collins. "Donna Reed: TV's Dearest Mom." *USA Today*, January 15, 1986, p. 2D.

B196. "Donna Reed, 64; 'Girl Next Door' Blossomed Into an Oscar Winner." *Chicago Tribune*, January 15, 1986.

B197. "Donna Reed Dead at 64." *New York Daily News*, January 15, 1986, p. 4.

B198. "Donna Reed Dies of Cancer at 64." *San Francisco Chronicle*, January 15, 1986, p. 4.

B199. "Film Actress Donna Reed, 1953 Oscar Winner, Dies." *Washington Post*, January 15, 1986, p. C4.

B200. Hoeschen, Kathy. "Just a 'Down-to-Earth Lady,' Says Brother." *Sioux City Journal*, January 15, 1986, p. A22.

B201. Ingrassia, Michele. "The All-American Girl." *New York Newsday*, January 15, 1986, Pt. II, p. 4-5.

B202. Kerr, Peter. "Donna Reed, Oscar Winner and a TV Star, Is Dead at 64." *New York Times*, January 15, 1986, p. B11.

B203. McCarthy, Todd. "Donna Reed, 64, Dies of Cancer; Oscar Winner Found TV Fame." *Daily Variety*, January 15, 1986. Reprinted in *Variety*, January 22, 1986, p. 4.

B204. McGillivray, David. Obituary. *Films and Filming* (England), March 1986, p. 47.

B205. "Milestones." *Time Magazine*, January 27, 1986, p. 78.

B206. Miller, Bruce R. "Denison's Donna Reed Dies at 64." *Sioux City Journal*, January 15, 1986, p. A22.

B207. "Miss Reed Maintained Iowa Ties Despite Success in Hollywood." *Omaha World-Herald*, January 15, 1986, p. 49.

B208. Moret, H. "Fondu au noir." *Revue de Cinema* (France), March 1986, p. 86-87.

B209. "Newsmakers." *Newsweek*, January 27, 1986, p. 72.

B210. Obituary. Classic Images, February 1986 (#128), p. 42.

B211. Obituary. Detroit Free Press, January 15, 1986.

B212. Obituary. Detroit News, January 15, 1986.

B213. Obituary. Facts On File, January 17, 1986 (vol. 46, No. 2356), p. 24.

B214. Obituary. Grand Angle (Belgium), February 1986, p. 45-46. Contains filmography.

B215. Obituary. The London Times, January 16, 1986.

B216. Osborne, Robert. Obituary. "Rambling Reporter" column. Hollywood Reporter, January 15, 1986, p. 1+.

B217. "Oscar-winning Star Donna Reed Dies of Cancer at 64." The Tampa Tribune (Tampa, Florida), January 15, 1986, p. 13B. Contains filmography.

B218. Seiler, Michael. "Donna Reed, Oscar Winner and TV Star, Dies at 64." Los Angeles Times, January 15, 1986, p. 3, 16.

B219. "The Television Generation Mourns Its Favorite Surrogate Mother, Rough But Tender Donna Reed." People Magazine, January 27, 1986, p. 84-86.

B220. Vilela, G. "Donna Reed, 1921-1986." Cinematographe (France), February 1986, p. 9.

Appreciation & Memorial

B221. Allen, Steve. "Two Donnas." Sioux City Journal, June 8, 1986, p. E1.

The actor pays tribute to the "Two Donnas" he knew: the sweet, small-town beauty and the outspoken woman of conviction and courage. Allen's only film with Donna was The Benny Goodman Story (see F36).

B222. Bulnes, J. "Les Immortels du Cinema: Donna Reed." Cine Revue (Belgium), January 30, 1986, p. 34-7. Contains biography and filmography.

B223. Caulfield, Deborah. "Donna Reed's Oscar Comes Home." Los Angeles Times, August 17, 1986.

Follows Donna Reed's Oscar to her home town, where she had decided it was to go. The pride of the residents of Denison in the star from their hometown is shown in other instances, i.e. the presentation by Denison High School's class of 1938 of a sign which reads "Denison, Hometown of Donna Reed." A photo of Bill Mullenger, Donna's brother, is shown.

B224. "Donna Reed Film Festival Attracts 'Devoted Legion.'" <u>Omaha World-Herald</u>, June 15, 1986.

B225. Fink, Mitchell. "Donna Reed's Friends Say Last Goodbyes to 'Classy Lady'." <u>Los Angeles Herald-Examiner</u>, January 18, 1986.

B226. Hitchens, Neal. "Donna Reed Was Killed by Larry Hagman & 'Dallas.'" <u>National Enquirer</u>, July 1989, p. 22.

Paul Petersen claims that the 'Dallas' ordeal-- and Larry Hagman in particular-- led to Donna's death. Petersen's post "Donna Reed Show" career and personal problems are discussed.

B227. Lyden, Pierce. "Action Shots: Donna Reed." <u>Classic Images</u> (Iowa), August 1986 (No. 134), p. 54.

Mr. Lyden, who worked on <u>The Get-Away</u> as a stunt driver, recalls his first impressions of Donna.

B228. Miller, Bruce R. "Reed's Oscar Sits in Brother's Office." <u>The Sioux City Journal</u>, March 21, 1986, p. A16.

Photo of Bill Mullenger holding the Academy Award accompanies the article.

B229. Miller, Bruce R. "Remembering Donna." <u>Sioux City Journal</u>, June 8, 1986, p. E1.

With B221, B231 & B235, comprised a special section devoted to Donna, leading up to the Donna Reed Film Festival.

B230. "Nick at Nite to air Donna-thon; hope seven-day rerun blitz will tidy the world." <u>Tampa Tribune-Times</u> (Tribune Wire Report), May 6, 1990, p. 10.

Report speculates on the "global impact" of 140 straight episodes of "The Donna Reed Show." (The week long "Donna-thon" aired in celebration of Mother's Day, 1990.)

B231. Osborne, Robert. "Rambling Reporter" column. <u>Hollywood Reporter</u>, June 5, 1986; March 31, 1988; June 9, 1988; March 27, 1989

In his column, Osborne reports regularly on the activities of the Donna Reed Foundation for the Performing Arts and the annual Donna Reed festival.

B232. Poole, Marcia. "Reed Never Forgot Her Iowa Roots."
       Sioux City Journal, June 8, 1986, p. E1.

B233. Quinlan, D.   "An Appreciation of Donna Reed."
       Photoplay (England, now Film Monthly), March 1986,
       p. 34-5.

B234. Raker, Al.   "Donna Reed: Sexy and Seductive."
       Hollywood Studio Magazine, March 1986, vol. 19,
       no. 3, p. 16-17.

B235. Scott, Vernon.   "Celebrities Gather to Eulogize
       Reed." New York Daily News, January 18, 1986.

B236. Welton, Michael.   "Denison Gears Up for Donna Reed
       Film Festival." Sioux City Journal, June 8, 1986,
       p. E1.

                          Book Excerpts

B237. Amory, Cleveland, ed. "Donna Reed." The Celebrity
       Register ("An Irreverent Compendium of American
       Quotable Notables").   New York: Harper & Row,
       1963, p. 512.

B238. Amory,   Cleveland,   ed.   "Donna   Reed."   The
       International Celebrity Register.   New York:
       Celebrity Register, Ltd., 1959, p. 613.

B239. Basinger, Jeanine. The "It's A Wonderful Life" Book.
       New York: Alfred A. Knopf, 1986, p. 9-12, 44.

B240. Brooks, Tim. "Donna Reed."   The Complete Directory
       to Prime Time TV Stars.   New York: Ballantine
       Books, 1987, p. 704.

B241. Burgess, Patricia, ed.   The Annual Obituary 1986.
       Chicago: St. James Press, 1989, p. 64-65.

B242. Chaneles, Sol and Albert Wolsky. The Movie Makers.
       Secaucus, N.J.: Derbibooks, Inc., 1974, p. 414.

B243. Eames, John Douglas.   The MGM Story: The Complete
       Story of 50 Roaring Years.   New York: Crown
       Publishing, 1975.

       Brief descriptions of all 1,705 MGM films.

B244. Eisner, Joel and David Krinsky.   "The Donna Reed
       Show" Television Comedy Series: An Episode Guide
       to 153 TV Sitcoms in Syndication. Jefferson,
       N.C.: McFarland & Co., Inc., 1984, p. 221-35.

       Brief descriptions and episode titles for each of
       the 274 episodes of "The Donna Reed Show."

B245. Gareffa, Peter, ed. "Donna Reed, 1921-1986." *Contemporary Newsmakers*, 1986 Cumulation. Detroit: Gale Research Company, 1987, p. 318.

B246. Grady, Billy. *The Irish Peacock: The Confessions of a Legendary Talent Agent*. New Rochelle, N.Y.: Arlington House, 1972.

B247. Halliwell, Leslie. "Donna Reed." *Halliwell's Filmgoer's Companion*, Ninth edition. New York: Charles Scribner's Sons, 1988, p. 582.

B248. Katz, Ephraim. "Donna Reed." *The Film Encyclopedia*. New York: Crowell Publishers, 1979, p. 955-956.

B249. Lamparski, Richard. *Whatever Became of..*, 5th series. New York: Crown, 1974, p. 170-1.

B250. McWilliams, Michael. "Donna Reed." *TV Sirens*. New York: Perigree Books, 1987, p. 135-36.

B251. Nash, Robert Jay and Stanley Ralph Ross. *The Motion Picture Guide, 1927-1983*. Chicago: Cinebooks, Inc., 1986, 10 volumes.

B252. O'Donnell, Monica M., ed. "Donna Reed." *Contemporary Theatre, Film and Television*, Vol. 3. Detroit: Gale Research Company, 1986, p. 311.

B253. Parish, James Robert and Ronald L. Bowers. "Donna Reed." *The Golden Era: The MGM Stock Company*. New Rochelle, N.Y.: Arlington House, 1973, p. 599-603.

B254. Ragan, David. "Donna Reed." *Movie Stars of the '40s*. Englewood Cliffs, N.J.: Prentice Hall, Inc., 1985, p. 177-78.

B255. Ragan, David. "Donna Reed." *Who's Who In Hollywood, 1900-1976*. New Rochelle, N.Y.: Arlington House, 1976, p. 380.

B256. Schuster, Mel. *Motion Picture Performers: A Bibliography of Magazine and Periodical Articles*, 1900-69. Metuchen, N.J.: Scarecrow Press, 1971, p. 553-4.

B257. Schuster, Mel. *Motion Picture Performers: A Bibliography of Magazine and Periodical Articles*, Supplement No. 1, 1970-1974. Metuchen, N.J.: Scarecrow Press, 1976, p. 608.

B258. Smith, John M. and Tim Cawkwell, ed. *World Encyclopedia of the Film*. New York: A & W Visual Library, 1972, p. 228.

B259. Thomas, Bob. *King Cohn: The Life and Times of Harry Cohn*. New York: G.P. Putnam's Sons, 1967.

B260. Thomson,   David.   "Donna   Reed."   Biographical
       Dictionary of Film. New York: William Morrow and
       Co., Inc., 1976, p. 469.

B261. Wiley, Mason and Damien Bona. Inside Oscar: The
       Unofficial History of the Academy Awards. New
       York: Ballantine Books, a Division of Random
       House, Inc., 1986, p. 238-243.

B262. Wine, Bill. "Donna Reed." Actors and Actresses: The
       International Directory of Films and Filmmakers:
       Volume III. James Vinson, ed. Chicago: St. James
       Press, 1986, p. 527-28.

Appendix:
The Donna Reed
Foundation and Festival

THE DONNA REED FOUNDATION FOR THE PERFORMING ARTS
1321 Broadway, P.O. Box 122, Denison, Iowa 51442
(712) 263-3334

Established in 1986, the Foundation is dedicated to the memory of Donna Reed, and its mission is to provide scholarship grants to students pursuing studies in the Performing Arts.

Each year, the Foundation sponsors the Donna Reed Festival, which takes place in Denison during the first weekend in June. The festival offers workshops taught by well-known personalities in the entertainment industry, as well as entertainment and social events. A highlight of the festival is the presentation of the Donna Reed Scholarship.

Serving on the Foundation's Board of Directors are Grover Asmus, Shelley Fabares, Penny Owen Stigers, Tony Owen Jr., Timothy Owen, and Mary Anne Owen. Among its Advisory Board are Howard Keel, Norma Connolly, Jimmy Hawkins, Paul Petersen and Ann McCrea Borden.

Index

Numbers preceded by "F" refer to entries in the Filmography section, "T" to Television Appearances, "DR" to "The Donna Reed Show" Episode Guide, "R" to Radio Appearances, "A" to Awards and Nominations, and "B" to the Bibliography. Numbers without a letter prefix are page numbers in the Biography or other sections without reference numbers.

About the Author

BRENDA SCOTT ROYCE is a freelance writer and performing arts researcher currently studying at the University of South Florida. She served as President of Star Data Research in New York from 1985 to 1988 and is a graduate of the Sarasota Visual and Performing Arts Center. She also served as research assistant for the book *Classic Sitcoms: A Celebration of the Best of Prime Time Comedies.*